How to Use This Book

Look for these special features in this book:

SIDEBARS, **CHARTS**, **GRAPHS**, and original **MAPS** expand your understanding of what's being discussed—and also make useful sources for classroom reports.

FAQs answer common **F**requently **A**sked **Q**uestions about people, places, and things.

WOW FACTORS offer "Who knew?" facts to keep you thinking.

TRAVEL GUIDE gives you tips on exploring the state—either in person or right from your chair!

PROJECT ROOM provides fun ideas for school assignments and incredible research projects. Plus, there's a guide to primary sources—what they are and how to cite them.

Please note: All statistics are as up-to-date as possible at the time of publication. Population data is taken from the 2010 census.

Consultant: William Harris Bragg, Professor of History and Geography, Georgia College and State University; Kris M. Irwin, Warnell School of Forestry and Natural Resources, University of Georgia; William Loren Katz; Kathleen Clark, Associate Professor, University of Georgia

Book production by The Design Lab

Library of Congress Cataloging-in-Publication Data
Prentzas, G. S.
  Georgia / by G. S. Prentzas. — Revised edition.
  pages cm. — (America the beautiful. Third series)
  Includes bibliographical references and index.
  ISBN 978-0-531-24881-2 (lib. bdg.)
  1. Georgia—Juvenile literature. I. Title.
  F286.3.P74 2014
  975.8—dc23   2013031924

1 2 3 4 5 6 7 8 9 10 R 23 22 21 20 19 18 17 16 15 14

AMERICA ★ THE ★ BEAUTIFUL

Georgia

BY G. S. PRENTZAS

Third Series, Revised Edition

Children's Press®
An Imprint of Scholastic Inc.
New York ★ Toronto ★ London ★ Auckland ★ Sydney
Mexico City ★ New Delhi ★ Hong Kong
Danbury, Connecticut

CONTENTS

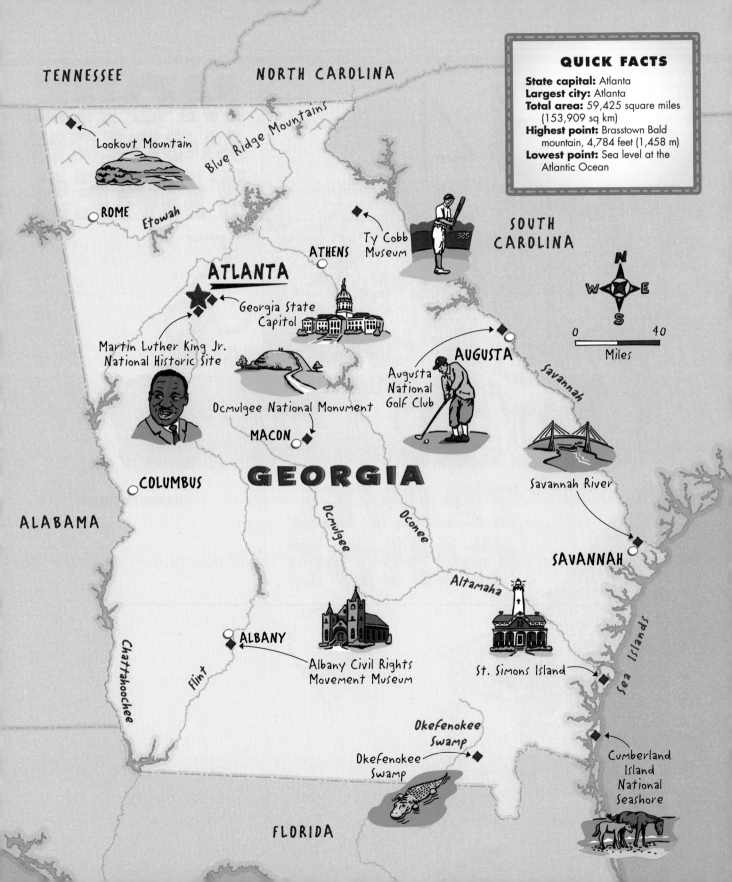

TENNESSEE

NORTH CAROLINA

Lookout Mountain

Blue Ridge Mountains

ROME

Etowah

Ty Cobb
Museum

ATHENS

SOUTH
CAROLINA

QUICK FACTS

State capital: Atlanta
Largest city: Atlanta
Total area: 59,425 square miles
(153,909 sq km)
Highest point: Brasstown Bald
mountain, 4,784 feet (1,458 m)
Lowest point: Sea level at the
Atlantic Ocean

N
W E
S

0   40
Miles

ATLANTA

Georgia State
Capitol

Martin Luther King Jr.
National Historic Site

AUGUSTA

Augusta
National
Golf Club

Savannah

Ocmulgee National Monument

MACON

GEORGIA

Savannah River

COLUMBUS

ALABAMA

Ocmulgee

Oconee

SAVANNAH

Altamaha

Chattahoochee

ALBANY

Flint

Albany Civil Rights
Movement Museum

St. Simons Island

Sea Islands

Okefenokee
Swamp

Okefenokee
Swamp

Cumberland
Island
National
Seashore

FLORIDA

Welcome to Georgia!

HOW DID GEORGIA GET ITS NAME?

In 1732, a group of wealthy men led by James Oglethorpe asked King George II of Great Britain for a large tract of land in North America. They wanted to start a new colony that would be settled by some of Britain's poor. The colony would give the less fortunate a chance to start a new life. The men asked the king for the land between the Altamaha and Savannah rivers in southeastern North America. The king granted the territory to Oglethorpe's group. It was the last of the 13 original British colonies to be founded. The colony was named the Province of Georgia, after the king.

GEORGIA

8

READ ABOUT

Georgia's Little
Grand Canyon
in Providence
Canyon State
Outdoor
Recreation Area

LAND LAND LAND LAND LAND

LAND

★

GEORGIA IS KNOWN AS THE PEACH STATE BECAUSE MANY PEACHES ARE GROWN THERE. But there's a lot more to Georgia than just peaches. Covering 59,425 square miles (153,909 square kilometers), Georgia is the second-largest state in the southeastern United States. With elevations ranging from sea level to more than 4,700 feet (1,400 meters), Georgia has rugged mountains, dense pine forests, alligator-filled swamps, and unspoiled coastal islands. A wide variety of plants and animals live in these varied environments.

WORDS TO KNOW

geologists *scientists who study rocks to find out what the earth is made of and how it has changed over time*

erosion *the gradual wearing away of rock or soil by physical breakdown, chemical solution, or water*

ROCK AND WATER

Many different natural forces have shaped Georgia's landscape. **Geologists** believe that the oldest rocks in Georgia date back more than 1 billion years. Some of these very old rocks are now Georgia's mountains. Over millions of years, **erosion** ate away at the mountains. Snowmelt and rainwater carried small bits of rock and minerals downhill. These tiny bits, called sediment, settled in what is now the Piedmont Plateau.

Until about 70 million years ago, the Atlantic Ocean covered much of Georgia. Find the cities of Augusta, Macon, and Columbus on a map. They would have been at the water's edge back then! Today, geologists find fossils of sea creatures such as mollusks and sand dollars many miles from Georgia's coast.

The ocean would eventually retreat to where it is now. During the glacial period of the last ice age (which ended about 10,000 years ago), temperatures were often very, very cold. Huge chunks of ice called glaciers spread through northern parts of North America. Glaciers never reached Georgia, but they still had a major effect on the state's land-

Georgia Geo-Facts

Along with the state's geographical highlights, this chart ranks Georgia's land, water, and total area compared to all other states.

Total area; rank	59,425 square miles (153,909 sq km); 24th
Land; rank	57,906 square miles (149,976 sq km); 21st
Water; rank	1,519 square miles (3,933 sq km); 25th
Inland water; rank	1,016 square miles (2,631 sq km); 20th
Coastal water; rank	48 square miles (124 sq km); 19th
Territorial water; rank	455 square miles (1,178 km); 15th
Geographic center	Twiggs County, 18 miles (29 km) southeast of Macon
Latitude	30° N to 35° N
Longitude	81° W to 85° W
Highest point	Brasstown Bald mountain, 4,784 feet (1,458 m)
Lowest point	Sea level at the Atlantic Ocean
Largest city	Atlanta
Longest river	Savannah River, 350 miles (563 km)

Source: U.S. Census Bureau, 2010 census

Georgia is larger than many countries, including Greece, Honduras, South Korea, and Malawi.

People enjoy the beach on Tybee Island outside Savannah.

scape. With so much water frozen into glaciers, there was less water in the oceans. Sea levels dropped worldwide, exposing more land. During warmer periods of the ice age, glaciers melted. Ocean levels rose again as more water returned to them.

Georgia's size grew and shrank, depending on the effect of glaciers on sea levels. Finally, temperatures leveled off. Georgia ended up much bigger than it had been before the ice age began.

LAND REGIONS

The states of Tennessee and North Carolina sit along Georgia's northern border. South Carolina lies to the northeast, and the waves of the Atlantic Ocean break along 100 miles (160 km) of Georgia's eastern side. Florida stretches along Georgia's southern border. To the west, Alabama shares a 291-mile (468 km) border with the Peach State.

Georgia has three main land regions: the mountain region, the Piedmont Plateau, and the coastal plain. Each region offers different experiences.

FAQ

Q8 WHERE DID GEORGIA'S SANDSTONE COME FROM?

A8 Sand-sized particles settled to the bottom of an ocean that covered Georgia more than 3 million years ago. The water and sediment pressing down turned the particles into sandstone.

FAQ

Q8 HOW DID THE BLUE RIDGE MOUNTAINS GET THEIR NAME?

A8 When viewed from far away, these mountains have a bluish color, especially on misty mornings.

The summit of Brasstown Bald mountain features a view of the Blue Ridge Mountains, as well as an information center and observation deck.

The Mountain Region

Georgia's mountain region has three sections: the Appalachian Plateau, the ridge and valley, and the Blue Ridge. The Appalachian Plateau, which stretches from New York to Alabama, includes a small slice of Georgia in the far northwestern corner of the state. This is a scenic area with sandstone cliffs and isolated valleys. The notable peaks in Georgia's Appalachian Plateau include Sand Mountain, Lookout Mountain, and Pigeon Mountain.

The ridge and valley region sits southeast of the Appalachian Plateau. It runs southwest from eastern Tennessee, through part of Georgia, and into eastern Alabama. As you can guess from its name, this region consists of many fertile valleys that lie between sandstone ridges.

The Blue Ridge Mountains extend from Pennsylvania to northwestern Georgia. They're part of the Appalachian Mountain Range. You'll find Georgia's tallest mountains in the Blue Ridge region, including the state's highest point. Brasstown Bald mountain rises 4,784 feet (1,458 m) above sea level.

The Piedmont Plateau

The Piedmont Plateau lies south of Georgia's mountain region. From its border with the mountain region, the Piedmont Plateau slowly slopes down from 1,500 feet (450 m) above sea level to about 400 feet (120 m) above sea level. There it meets the coastal plain. The Piedmont Plateau's gentle, rolling hills cover about 30 percent of the state. Much of Georgia's most fertile farmland is located here.

A series of low ridges run southwest from Augusta in the eastern part of the state to Columbus in the western part. These ridges separate the Piedmont Plateau from the coastal plain. This dramatic change in landscape is called the fall line. Along these ridges, rivers flowing from the higher elevations of the Piedmont fall sharply to the lower coastal plain, creating waterfalls and rapids. The waterfalls and rapids prevent boats

The Minnehaha Falls are in Rabun County in northeastern Georgia.

The Piedmont is named after a region at the foot of the Alps mountain system in Italy. The name literally means "foot" (*piede*) of the "mountain" (*monte*).

from traveling any farther upstream. Long ago, people and goods traveling down Georgia's major rivers were transferred from boats to wagons (and later to trains) before the waters got rough. Cities sprouted up at these transfer points.

Georgia's Topography

Use the color-coded elevation chart to see on the map Georgia's high points (dark red to orange) and low points (green to dark green). Elevation is measured as the distance above or below sea level.

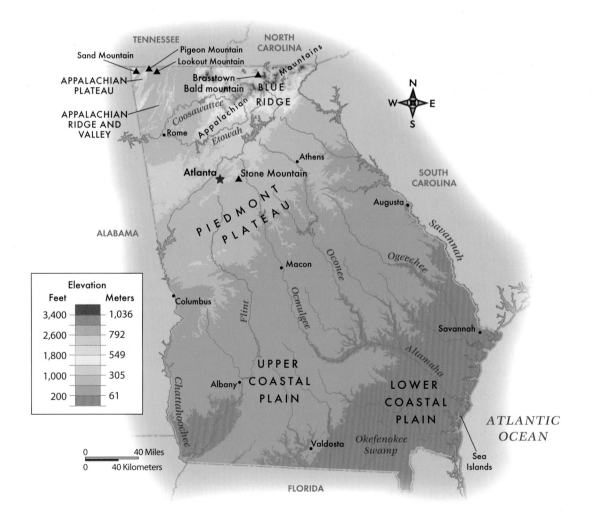

THE COASTAL PLAIN

The coastal plain covers the entire southern half of Georgia. It is part of the Atlantic Plain, which stretches along the East Coast of the United States from Massachusetts to Florida and west along the Gulf of Mexico. Georgia's coastal plain consists of two sections: the upper coastal plain and the lower coastal plain. It is Georgia's largest region, covering about 60 percent of the state.

The upper coastal plain lies in central and southwestern Georgia. It runs from the fall line south to Florida and east to within about 65 miles (105 km) of the Atlantic Ocean. The upper coastal plain's soil is less sandy than the lower coastal plain's soil. Here farmers grow crops such as peanuts, vegetables, and cotton.

The lower coastal plain includes the state's lowest elevations: the coastal area, the Okefenokee Swamp, and the **barrier islands**. The region is mostly flat with sandy soil. It has many marshes, swamps, and other wetlands. The Okefenokee Swamp is the second-largest freshwater swamp in the United States. It's a **bog** composed of islands, lakes, and prairies that covers 950 square miles (2,460 sq km). Okefenokee's name comes from the Choctaw Indian phrase meaning "land of the trembling earth." Throughout the swamp are large clumps of peat—the material formed by the decay of plants in water. They're unstable and will shake like gelatin when walked on. The murky brown color of the swamp water comes from decaying peat and plants.

WORDS TO KNOW

barrier islands *islands that are created by the gradual buildup of sand and stones from the ocean floor*

bog *an area of wet, marshy ground where the soil consists mostly of decomposing plant material*

SEE IT HERE!

OKEFENOKEE SWAMP

Okefenokee Swamp is like no other place on earth. It's home to lots of interesting and unusual plants, including water lilies, bladderworts, and pitcher plants (which eat insects!). Cypress, blackgum, and pine trees also grow in the swamp. Scientists have counted 233 different kinds of birds, 49 different mammals, 64 different reptiles, 37 different amphibians, and 39 different fish in Okefenokee. These include American bald eagles, otters, snakes, and the swamp's most famous residents—alligators.

GEORGIAITES

Georgiaites are round, greenish pieces of natural glass found in the soil of Georgia's coastal plain. Although nobody is certain how Georgiaites were created, many scientists believe that they were produced when an asteroid or comet hit Earth. The impact could have caused Earth rock to melt and fly into the air (imagine throwing a big rock into a lake and watching the drops of water splash up). The Georgiaites are the small pieces of molten rock that cooled as they fell back to Earth.

Ocean tides, sand, and river silt have worked together to create the Sea Islands, a string of more than 100 barrier islands off the coasts of South Carolina, Georgia, and northern Florida. They are called barrier islands because they form a barrier between the sea and the mainland. Sand, wind, waves, currents, and tides continue to change the shape of Georgia's barrier islands.

CLIMATE

Georgia has a mostly moderate climate. The warm waters of the nearby Atlantic Ocean and Gulf of Mexico usually keep the temperatures mild. Dogwoods, magnolias, azaleas, and other plants bloom during the warm days of spring. Except in the mountains, summer is hot and often humid, especially along the coast. In fall, Georgia's forests are filled with the colors of autumn. Winter is cool and occasionally cold.

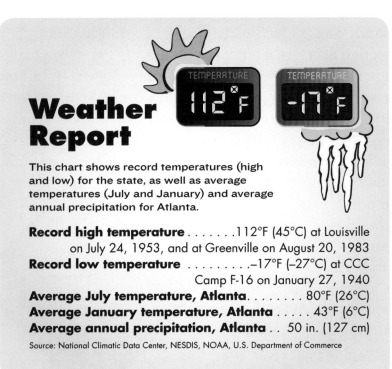

TEMPERATURE **112°F**   TEMPERATURE **-17°F**

Weather Report

This chart shows record temperatures (high and low) for the state, as well as average temperatures (July and January) and average annual precipitation for Atlanta.

Record high temperature . . . . . . .112°F (45°C) at Louisville on July 24, 1953, and at Greenville on August 20, 1983
Record low temperature . . . .–17°F (–27°C) at CCC Camp F-16 on January 27, 1940
Average July temperature, Atlanta. . . . . . . 80°F (26°C)
Average January temperature, Atlanta . . . . . 43°F (6°C)
Average annual precipitation, Atlanta . . 50 in. (127 cm)

Source: National Climatic Data Center, NESDIS, NOAA, U.S. Department of Commerce

About 40 to 50 inches (100 to 127 centimeters) of rain falls on Georgia each year. The mountains average about four light snowfalls a year. Farther south, the Piedmont occasionally has snow, sleet, freezing rain, and ice storms. In summer and fall, tropical storms dump buckets of rain on the state, and an occasional hurricane will batter the coast.

PLANT LIFE

Georgia has nearly 25 million acres (10 million hectares) of forests, more than any other southern state. Half of Georgia's forests are pine, about one-third are hardwood (such as oak, hickory, and cypress), and the rest are a mix of pine and hardwood trees. Peach and pecan trees have been planted in many parts of the state. Georgia is also home to one of the world's rarest trees, the Franklin tree. The shrublike tree grows about 20 feet (6 m) tall and has large white flowers. The Franklin tree no longer grows in the wild but can be cultivated. In spring and summer, dogwoods and magnolias flower throughout the state.

THE SEA ISLANDS HURRICANE

Georgia has a short coastline compared to other Atlantic and Gulf coast states, so it has suffered less destruction from hurricanes, powerful storms that develop at sea. In August 1893, however, a devastating hurricane came ashore near Savannah. Known as the Sea Islands Hurricane, it was one of the deadliest hurricanes in U.S. history. The storm killed as many as 2,000 people in Georgia and South Carolina.

Forests cover about two-thirds of Georgia.

Azaleas and moss-covered trees line a path in Savannah.

Georgia National Park Areas

This map shows some of Georgia's national parks, monuments, preserves, and other areas protected by the National Park Service.

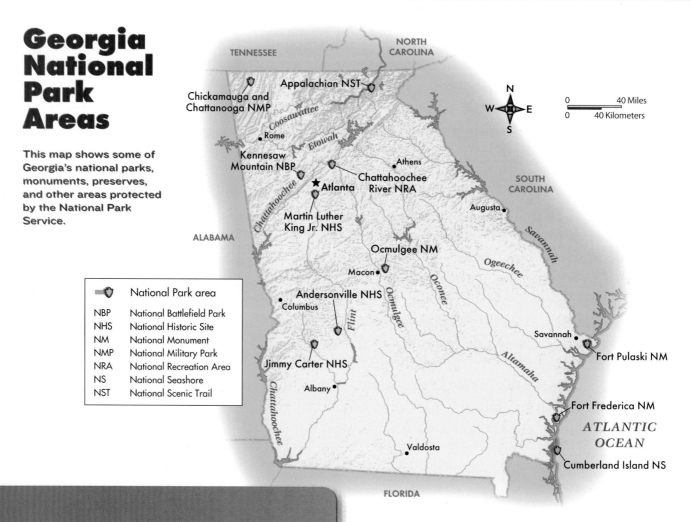

TENNESSEE

NORTH CAROLINA

Chickamauga and Chattanooga NMP

Appalachian NST

Coosawattee

Rome

Etowah

Kennesaw Mountain NBP

Athens

Chattahoochee River RA

Chattahoochee

★ Atlanta

SOUTH CAROLINA

Augusta

Savannah

Martin Luther King Jr. NHS

ALABAMA

Ocmulgee NM

Macon

Ogeechee

Oconee

Andersonville NHS

Columbus

Ocmulgee

Flint

Savannah

Altamaha

Fort Pulaski NM

Jimmy Carter NHS

Fort Frederica NM

Albany

ATLANTIC OCEAN

Chattahoochee

Valdosta

Cumberland Island NS

FLORIDA

N W E S

0 — 40 Miles
0 — 40 Kilometers

	National Park area
NBP	National Battlefield Park
NHS	National Historic Site
NM	National Monument
NMP	National Military Park
NRA	National Recreation Area
NS	National Seashore
NST	National Scenic Trail

ENDANGERED ANIMALS

The U.S. Fish and Wildlife Service lists 49 animal species in Georgia as endangered or threatened. Among the threatened or endangered birds that live in Georgia are the piping plover and the wood stork. Threatened or endangered fish and reptiles include the shortnose sturgeon, the eastern indigo snake, and the hawksbill sea turtle. Two types of whales, two kinds of bats, and the West Indian manatee are endangered mammals that live in Georgia or its coastal waters.

Piping plover

ANIMAL LIFE

Lots of different kinds of animals can be found in Georgia. White-tailed deer live throughout the state. Raccoons, opossums, and cottontail rabbits are also common. Three different types of squirrels—gray, fox, and flying—live in the state. Black bears are often spotted in Georgia's mountains and in the Okefenokee Swamp. Common birds include sparrows, robins,

A baby loggerhead turtle

and the brown thrasher (the state bird). Wild turkeys and quail live on the Piedmont and coastal plain. Along the coast and in marshes, sandhill pipers, snowy egrets, and other wading birds fish for their dinners. Ospreys build their impressive nests close to water so they can catch their favorite meal—fish. Sea animals, from dolphins to crabs, are found off of Georgia's coast.

Georgia is home to many types of reptiles and amphibians. The state's poisonous snakes include copperheads, eastern rattlesnakes, and cottonmouths (or water moccasins). Alligators stalk prey in the Okefenokee Swamp and other marshlands. Georgia has more salamander species than anywhere else in the world.

Wild turkeys roam on Cumberland Island.

LOGGERHEAD TURTLES

There are only seven different species of sea turtles in the world. Five of them search for food along Georgia's coast. And one—the loggerhead—nests on Georgia's Sea Islands. Loggerheads, like all sea turtles, live at sea but come ashore to lay eggs. Loggerhead turtles grow to about 3 feet long (1 m) and weigh about 200 pounds (90 kilograms).

The loggerhead is a threatened species. In the past, people caught loggerheads for their meat and shells. Today, the turtles often die when they are caught up in fishing nets or struck by boat propellers. Some also die from swallowing plastic bags, which look a lot like one of their favorite foods: jellyfish. Hogs, raccoons, and dogs often eat loggerhead eggs and gobble up hatchlings. Laws protect the loggerheads' hatching grounds on the Sea Islands. Two groups, the Jekyll Island Sea Turtle Project and the Brunswick Sea Turtle Movement Study, watch loggerhead nests. They scare away animals looking for a meal and make sure newborn turtles reach the sea.

MINI-BIO

LEON NEEL: FRIEND OF THE FOREST

Forest expert Leon Neel (1927–) believes that loggers should cut down individual trees for timber, instead of cutting down all the trees in a forest. This approach to forestry, called the Stoddard-Neel method, provides lumber while allowing forests and the wildlife that live in them to thrive. An authority on Georgia's longleaf pine forests, Neel has helped save many old stands of trees in the state.

? Want to know more? Visit www.factsfornow .scholastic.com and enter the keyword **Georgia**.

HUMANS AND THE ENVIRONMENT

People have had a major impact on Georgia's environment. Rice and cotton farms exhausted the soil, which led to erosion. Loggers stripped many forests of their trees. Longleaf pines throughout the state were cut down for lumber and pine gum, and lumberjacks cut down cypress trees in the Okefenokee Swamp, throughout the early 20th century. By the 1960s, industry had polluted the state's air and waterways.

Today, the biggest threat to the state's environment is population growth. Georgia is the fastest-growing state east of the Rocky Mountains.

Loggers cut down trees near the Okefenokee Swamp.

More people means more pollution. Population growth also leads to the destruction of **habitats**. New houses, roads, and shopping centers are built where forests and fields once were. Across the state, almost 400,000 acres (161,000 ha) of forest were lost to development between 2001 and 2005. Many Georgians are working hard to protect animals that are in danger of disappearing if their habitats and food supplies are not preserved.

New developments have replaced forests that once covered the land near Atlanta in Fulton County, Georgia.

WORD TO KNOW

habitats *places where animals or plants naturally live*

READ ABOUT

The Rock Eagle
Mound in
Eatonton, Georgia

c. 10,000 BCE ▲
*The first humans
arrive in Georgia*

c. 3000 BCE
*Native Americans in
Georgia begin building
permanent settlements
along waterways*

c. 300 BCE–
600 CE
*Native Americans in
Georgia begin building
earthen and rock mounds*

CHAPTER TWO

FIRST PEOPLE

★

WOULD YOU BELIEVE THAT PEOPLE HAVE LIVED IN GEORGIA FOR ABOUT 12,000 YEARS? Scientists think that the first humans arrived in North America as long as 20,000 years ago. At the time, a 1,000-mile-wide (1,600 km) strip of land connected what are now Russia and Alaska. People probably walked from Asia to North America to hunt game animals.

c. 800 CE
The Mississippian culture begins

c. 1350 ▲
The Mississippian culture fades, and Native peoples live in smaller groups

c. 1700
The Creek and Cherokee nations had formed

Archaeologists dig for artifacts near Jacksonville.

WORDS TO KNOW

archaeologists *people who study the remains of past human societies*

artifacts *objects remaining from a particular period of time*

WHO WERE THE NATIVE GEORGIANS?

The descendants of these Asian hunters gradually spread throughout North and South America. They arrived in what is now Georgia about 12,000 years ago. They found an area with mild weather and plenty of sunshine. Its fertile soil, dense forests, and many streams supported much plant and animal life. It was a good place to live.

Not much is known about the people who first settled Georgia. **Archaeologists** have found little evidence of these societies except for some spear points and a few skeletons. By looking at early **artifacts** discovered in other southeastern states, however, scientists can imagine how the first Georgians lived. They believe that people lived in small groups, or bands, of 20 to 50 people. These bands hunted huge ice age mammals like mastodons and sloths, soon to become extinct, as well as smaller animals. They also gathered nuts, fruits, berries, and other edible plants.

Native American Peoples
(Before European Contact)

This map shows the general area of Native American peoples before European settlers arrived.

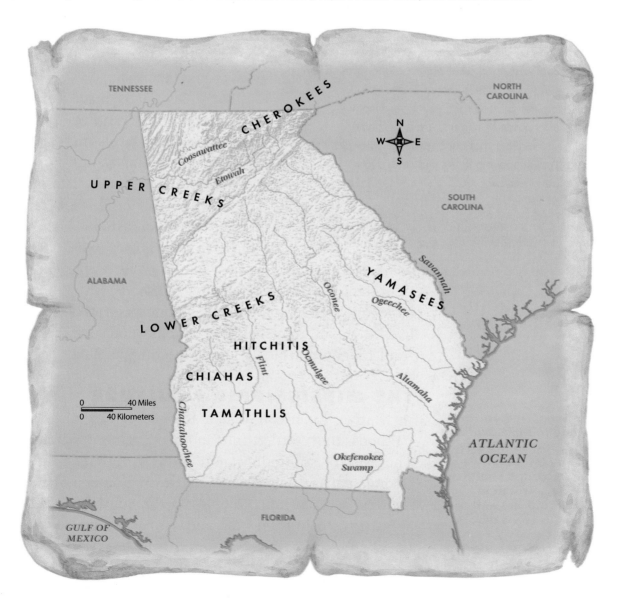

Picture Yourself . . .

Building a Wattle and Daub House

What if you had to build your own home without lumber and power tools? That's what early Georgians had to do. They built houses using natural materials that they found around them.

Building a house takes time and skill. You first have to chop down young trees and cut off the branches to make the trunks into poles. Then you have to dig a bunch of holes or a long trench in the shape of the house you want. You make the house's framework by standing up each wooden pole in a separate hole or side by side in the trench. Walls are made by weaving branches, vines, and other plant material around the poles. This type of woven wall is known as a wattle. To protect the walls from the sun and rain, you cover them with daub, a type of plaster made from mud, straw, and other materials. Finally, you make a roof out of straw or other plant material, leaving a small opening in the middle to allow smoke from your fire to escape.

Native Georgians lived on Stallings Island in the Savannah River about 3,500 to 4,500 years ago. They left behind a giant pile of discarded shellfish shells that today stretches across 2 acres (0.8 ha) and is 10 feet (3 m) high in some places.

Archaeologists believe that these people did not stay in one place for long. They moved to hunt animals or collect foods that were available only at certain spots during specific times of the year. Early Georgians usually traveled by foot, but they sometimes paddled the streams and rivers in canoes and other wooden boats. Their houses were built from reeds, bark, grasses, and other plants.

Early Georgians made stone spear points for hunting. They also used stone tools to carve wood, prepare food, and strip animal hides to make leather. They likely made other tools out of bone, wood, and shell.

Between 3,000 and 5,000 years ago, the population began to grow. As the early Georgians developed farming methods, they built larger, more permanent villages along waterways. They lived in small, rectangular or circular houses, ranging from 12 feet (4 m) to 30 feet (9 m) long per side.

THE MISSISSIPPIAN CULTURE

As Native American bands learned better farming methods, they settled into more permanent villages. They also began trading more often with other bands. Georgia natives may have traded with groups living as far west as Louisiana. Peoples in the Southeast probably began using the bow and arrow around 700 CE. Bows and arrows made hunting much easier. They also made warfare more deadly and more common. Archaeologists believe that Native Americans began protecting their villages with wooden fences at about the same time that arrow points arrived in Georgia.

The growth of agriculture and the increased threat of warfare led to a new way of life. Small settlements eventually became large, impressive villages. These villages were the heart of a new civilization known as the Mississippian culture. From 800 to 1600, people living in what are now the southern and midwestern United States belonged to some of the most complex societies that ever existed in North America.

The Mississippians were highly skilled farmers. Using simple tools, they grew corn, beans, squash, pumpkins, tobacco, and other plants. Men and women worked together to plant and harvest the crops. In between planting and harvest, women tended the crops and gathered fruits, nuts, and other foods. Men fished and hunted animals. The Mississippians wove baskets and made clay pottery in which to store their food.

By the 1500s, Native Americans in Georgia had more than 40 different ways to prepare corn, including roasting, boiling, and grinding it into cornmeal.

Native Americans hunting deer. Some wore deerskins as disguises, to trick the animals.

Carvings from Etowah Indian Mounds Historic Site

SEE IT HERE!

ETOWAH INDIAN MOUNDS

The most impressive American Indian mounds in Georgia are at Etowah Indian Mounds Historic Site near Cartersville in northwestern Georgia. Native Americans lived there from about the 12th century until the 17th century. Today, the park includes seven mounds, a plaza, part of the original village, and a museum. You can walk to the top of the central mound, which is 60 feet (18 m) tall. The mound is the highest point in the area, so the plaza, the other mounds, and the Etowah River are all visible.

The Mississippians built large villages close to rivers or streams. The best soil for growing crops was located along these waterways, which also provided a source of water and easy transportation routes. The typical village had a central plaza surrounded by homes and other buildings.

Each village was organized into two groups: the elites (or nobility) and the commoners. The elites consisted of a small number of people belonging to the same family. Elites were believed to be descended from the gods and to have supernatural powers. They lived in larger houses, wore special clothes, and ate different food than the commoners. The elites performed religious duties but did not work. Commoners grew all the food and served as warriors and workers.

MOUND BUILDERS

Native societies during this era developed religious ceremonies that involved building temples and burial mounds made of earth. The Mississippians burned the bodies of their dead and then placed the ashes in earthen or rock mounds. The earliest mounds in Georgia are small domes that served as graves. They date back more than 2,000 years. Later, workers built mounds as tall as 100 feet (30 m). Most of these mounds were built gradually, sometimes over 100 years. The mounds had different uses. Some were cemeteries for the elite. Others served as platforms for the homes of chiefs or as stages for religious ceremonies.

Between about 1350 and 1500, the large Native American villages in the Southeast broke apart. Growing populations, crop failures, and political disagreements weakened the villages' ruling families. Smaller groups, or tribes, split off and settled in many of Georgia's river valleys. European explorers and settlers would later call these peoples Hitchitis, Chiahas, Tamathlis, and Yamassees, among others.

LIFE AFTER THE EUROPEANS

The first Europeans known to have set foot in Georgia arrived at the mouth of the Savannah River, near what is now the state's border with South Carolina, on May 3, 1525. They were aboard two Spanish ships exploring the eastern coast of North America. From 1539 to 1542, Spanish general Hernando de Soto and his army traveled through the Southeast in search of riches. Some of de Soto's men wrote descriptions of Native groups that controlled large areas. Coosas, Ichisis, and Ocutes were the largest and most powerful of these groups.

When Europeans began establishing small settlements in Georgia in the 16th century, many Native Americans moved to be closer to European villages in order to trade with the newcomers. These native people later joined together to form two major groups: Creeks and Cherokees. Creeks lived in parts of present-day Alabama, Tennessee, and central and southern Georgia. Europeans called them Creeks because they lived in villages along waterways. Creeks called themselves Muskogees. Cherokees lived in the Blue Ridge Mountains in what is now North Carolina, Tennessee, and northern Georgia. Soon, however, disease, war, and disputes over land would push the Creek and Cherokee nations out of Georgia.

ENCOUNTERING GEORGIA'S NATIVE PEOPLES

"[The chief] awaited us in peace in his town. We made much festivity for him when we arrived and jousted and had many horse races, although he appeared to think little of all this. Afterward we asked him to give us Indians to carry the burdens, and he responded that he was not accustomed to serving anyone, rather that all served him before."
—Luys Hernández de Biedma, a member of the de Soto expedition

A Creek necklace made of animal teeth and bone

READ ABOUT

Hernando de Soto leads an expedition in search of gold through southeastern North America.

1566 ▲

Spanish admiral Pedro Menéndez de Avilés explores the Georgia coast

1721 ▲

Fort King George, the first British settlement in Georgia, is built

1733

James Oglethorpe and 120 colonists arrive in Georgia

EXPLORATION AND SETTLEMENT

★

I N 1539, MORE THAN 600 SPANISH SOL-DIERS LED BY HERNANDO DE SOTO MARCHED INLAND FROM FLORIDA'S WESTERN COAST. In March 1540, they crossed the Ochlockonee River, entering what is now southern Georgia. The Spaniards pushed northeast, crossing the Savannah River not far from present-day Augusta, Georgia. They wandered through much of southeastern North America.

1750
Slavery is legalized in Georgia

1776 ▲
Three Georgians sign the Declaration of Independence

1782
The British leave Georgia forever

European Exploration of Georgia

The colored arrows on this map show the route taken by de Soto between 1540 and 1541.

SPANISH GEORGIA

During their travels, many of de Soto's men died in battles with the Native Americans or from illnesses. De Soto died of a fever in 1542. The rest of his men returned to Mexico, which was a Spanish colony at the time.

In 1565, Spanish admiral Pedro Menéndez de Avilés constructed a fort at present-day St. Augustine, Florida. It was the first permanent European settlement in what is now the United States. The following year, Menéndez explored and mapped the coastlines of present-day Georgia and South Carolina. He constructed forts on three of the Sea Islands—Cumberland, Sapelo, and St. Simons. The newcomers in each **colony** soon set up churches. Priests introduced many Native Americans to the Catholic faith.

Over the next two centuries, Spain, France, and England claimed what is now Georgia as their own territory. As more and more Europeans arrived, the relationship between the newcomers and Native Americans became tense. Battles over land killed people on both sides. Even more Native Americans died from European diseases, such as measles and smallpox. Because these diseases had been common in Europe for centuries, many Europeans had built up **immunity** to them. But Native Americans had never been exposed to these diseases, so their bodies could not fight them. European diseases spread quickly through

In 1568, a Spanish priest living in what is now Georgia translated a religious book into Guale, the language of the people of the Sea Islands. Historians believe that it was the first book written in what is now the United States.

WORDS TO KNOW

colony *a community settled in a new land but with ties to another government*

immunity *natural protection against disease*

Smallpox and other diseases proved deadly for Native Americans throughout North America.

Native American villages. To escape the disease and the fighting, Native Americans started moving inland, away from European settlements.

England established its first colony in North America at Jamestown, Virginia, in 1607 and then expanded its colonies southward. King Charles II awarded the large region called Carolina to eight of his supporters in 1663. They established Charles Town (now Charleston in present-day South Carolina) as the capital of the Carolina Colony. The land located between the Spaniards in Florida and the British in Carolina soon attracted attention. Both European powers sought to expand into this territory. Each side tried to establish friendly relations with Creeks and Cherokees who lived there.

When Native Americans attacked Spain's Sea Island forts in the 1680s, the Spanish retreated back to Florida. British colonists from South Carolina took advantage of the Spaniards' departure. They began settling on Native lands in what is now Georgia. In 1715, a Creek chief known as Emperor Brim attacked these new English settlements. He chased the Europeans back to Charles Town. The Carolina colonists demanded that King George I provide troops to protect them. In 1721, the British built Fort King George near present-day Darien, Georgia. At the time, it was the southernmost outpost of Great Britain's North American colonies.

OGLETHORPE'S NOBLE EXPERIMENT

The 1720s were hard times for many British people. They could not find work and ended up in debt. In Great Britain at the time, if you did not pay your bills, you could be sent to jail. An influential lawmaker named James Oglethorpe wanted to find a way to provide jobs

General Oglethorpe meets a group of Creeks in 1733.

for the poor. In 1730, he led a group that sent a petition to King George II. They asked for land in North America to establish a new colony. They requested the land between the Altamaha and Savannah rivers, which had been claimed by both Spain and Great Britain.

Under Oglethorpe's plan, a group of Britain's poor would settle the colony. Moving to North America would give them the chance to improve their lives. Oglethorpe proposed that the colony be named the Province of Georgia, in honor of the king. George II approved the idea. He reasoned that the new colony would increase British trade with North America. It would also help protect British colonists in South Carolina. They feared attacks by Spanish troops from Florida or by American Indians. On June 9, 1732, the king granted a charter for the new colony. He appointed Oglethorpe and his partners to oversee the new colony. The Trustees, as they were known, used their connections to raise money and supplies for Georgia.

BETWEEN TWO CULTURES

The daughter of a British trader and a Creek mother, Mary Musgrove (c. 1700–c. 1763) grew up speaking both English and Creek. She and her husband set up a trading post near the Savannah River. When James Oglethorpe arrived in Georgia in 1733, he hired Mary Musgrove as an interpreter. She translated English to the Creek language (and vice versa), making sure everyone understood each other. She also taught Oglethorpe about Creek ways.

An engraving of Savannah in 1734, a year after it was founded

Oglethorpe wanted to fill the colony with poor, honest people who had been released from debtors' prison. But people from all walks of life sought to join Oglethorpe in North America. Hundreds applied for the voyage. Oglethorpe selected people he thought would be useful. Carpenters, farmers, merchants, and a doctor were among the original colonists. Oglethorpe did not choose a single debtor, and in fact, few debtors ever made it to the colony that had been created for them.

Oglethorpe and 120 colonists left Great Britain in November 1732. After a wave-tossed voyage across the Atlantic, their ship arrived at Beaufort, South Carolina, the following January. Robert Johnson, the governor of the Carolina Colony, provided the newcomers with farm animals, tools, boats, and other supplies to help them get started. Oglethorpe traveled south to find a suitable site for the settlement. He chose a spot overlooking the Savannah River. Yamacraw Bluff was on high ground, making it easy to defend. It was also close to South Carolina and its supplies. Oglethorpe returned with all of the colonists to the site, which would become known as Savannah, on February 1, 1733.

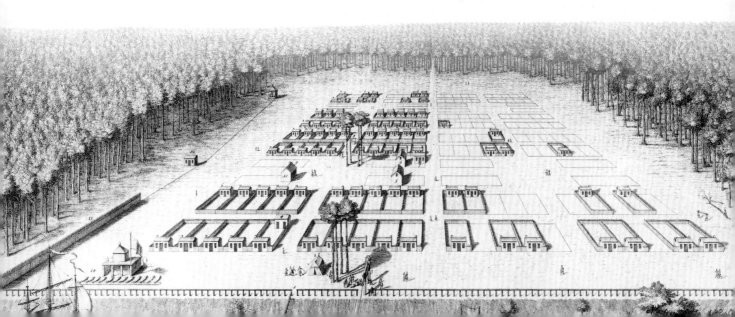

Georgia's first colonists immediately began work. They chopped down trees and used them to build houses. Oglethorpe soon signed a treaty with Creeks that allowed the colonists to settle on Native American land.

The Georgia Colony struggled from the very beginning. Oglethorpe wanted the colony to produce silk, a profitable product at the time. Silk is made from the cocoons of silkworms, which eat mulberry leaves. Oglethorpe ordered 10 mulberry trees planted on each acre of cleared land. Unfortunately, the silkworms didn't like the mulberry tree leaves that grew in Georgia. The colonists also planted grapes, oranges, and olives, but these crops fared poorly in Georgia's soil and climate.

For the next 50 years, Georgia floundered. The colony survived mainly because the British government provided money and supplies. New towns were settled, however. Augusta was built 140 miles (225 km) upstream from Savannah, and Frederica was established on St. Simons Island. In 1715 and 1740, the British used Georgia as a base to launch attacks against their Spanish enemies in Florida. In 1742, Spanish troops fought back, attacking Frederica. British forces fended off the attack. The Spaniards retreated to Florida, leaving Georgia forever.

SLAVERY IN COLONIAL GEORGIA

Oglethorpe and the Trustees had banned slavery because they wanted Georgia to be a place for British people to start a new and free life. During the 1740s, however, wealthy colonists ignored the law and smuggled in enslaved people to work on their large farms and rice plantations.

By 1749, Oglethorpe had resigned as a trustee. He went back to England, never to return to the colony. Georgia's illegal slave owners successfully pressured the colony's leaders to end the ban on slavery. In 1750, fewer than 500

SEE IT HERE!

FORT FREDERICA

Fort Frederica, which sits on St. Simons Island, played an important role in Georgia's history. In 1742, about 5,000 Spanish troops attempted to seize this new British colony. British troops led by James Oglethorpe defeated the Spaniards at Fort Frederica. The victory ensured that Georgia would remain a British colony. Today, you can visit the remnants of the fort and learn about the battle at Fort Frederica National Monument.

NANCY HART: REVOLUTIONARY WAR HEROINE

Nancy Hart (1735-1830) was Georgia's most famous female figure during the Revolutionary War (1775-1783). Bold and courageous, she was usually alone at home with her children while her husband served in the Georgia army. She often disguised herself as a man to spy on British soldiers stationed in Georgia. In one often-told story, she bested six British soldiers who had invaded her home, shooting two and holding the others prisoner until her husband arrived. Hart's feisty temper and bright red hair earned her the nickname "war woman" from local Cherokees.

Want to know more? Visit www.factsfornow .scholastic.com and enter the keyword **Georgia**.

enslaved people lived in Georgia. By the American Revolution, Georgia was home to more than 18,000 enslaved people—almost half the colony's population. Enslaved fieldworkers toiled from dawn to dusk.

In 1754, the British government took control of the colony from the Trustees. John Reynolds was appointed Georgia's first governor. During these years, Georgia grew faster than any other British colony.

REVOLUTION

Meanwhile, colonists continued to pour into Georgia and settle on Native American lands. The American Indians resisted. Great Britain sent in troops to defend the colonists. The British thought the colonists should help pay for the troops. But the colonists became outraged at the new taxes that were imposed because they argued that only their elected assemblies could tax them. Tensions grew between Great Britain and the colonies. Some colonists began to think that they should break away from Britain. Rebellion was in the air.

Many Georgians, however, remained loyal to the British. The youngest colony was dependent on Great Britain for money, supplies, and protection from Native Americans. Many wealthy Georgians also had strong economic ties to England.

The American Revolution began in April 1775. In Georgia, colonists who supported independence established the Council of Safety, which seized control of the colony's government. Governor James Wright left Georgia in January 1776. Three delegates from Georgia—Button Gwinnett, Lyman Hall, and George Walton—signed the Declaration of Independence that July. The 13 English colonies were now 13 independent states. Georgia adopted its own **constitution** in 1777 and set up its own government.

Except for a few skirmishes between Georgian Patriots and British Loyalists from Florida, the Revolutionary War at first hardly touched Georgia during the early years of the conflict. Then in 1779, British troops seized Savannah and much of lower Georgia. The Patriots still controlled upper Georgia. Governor Wright returned to Savannah and announced that Georgia had been restored to British rule.

The American Patriots slowly recaptured all of Georgia. In October 1781, Georgians received news that the British army had surrendered at Yorktown, Virginia. The following July, Governor Wright and British troops abandoned Savannah. In 1783, the United States and Great Britain signed the Treaty of Paris, which recognized the independence of the United States. Georgia was now part of a new, free country.

Great Britain regained control of only one of its 13 colonies during the American Revolution. That one was Georgia.

WORD TO KNOW

constitution *a written document that contains all the governing principles of a state or country*

British soldiers, who wore red coats, attack American troops in Savannah during the Revolutionary War.

READ ABOUT

George
Washington
(standing on step)
presiding at the
Constitutional
Convention
in 1787

1793 ▲

Eli Whitney invents the
cotton gin, making cotton
farming profitable

▲ 1838

Cherokees are forced
out of Georgia on the
Trail of Tears

1861

Georgia secedes
from the Union

CHAPTER FOUR

GROWTH AND CHANGE

★

IN 1787, FOUR DELEGATES FROM GEORGIA ATTENDED THE CONSTITUTIONAL CONVENTION IN PHILADELPHIA. They joined delegates from other states to write the U.S. Constitution. Then Georgia voted to ratify, or approve, the Constitution on January 2, 1788, becoming the nation's fourth state.

1864 ▶
Union general William T. Sherman leads a destructive march from Atlanta to Savannah

1867
Georgia is placed under military control during Reconstruction

1915
A boll weevil infestation destroys cotton crops

Georgia: From Territory to Statehood
(1732–1788)

This map shows the original Georgia territory and the area (outlined in red)
that became the state of Georgia in 1788.

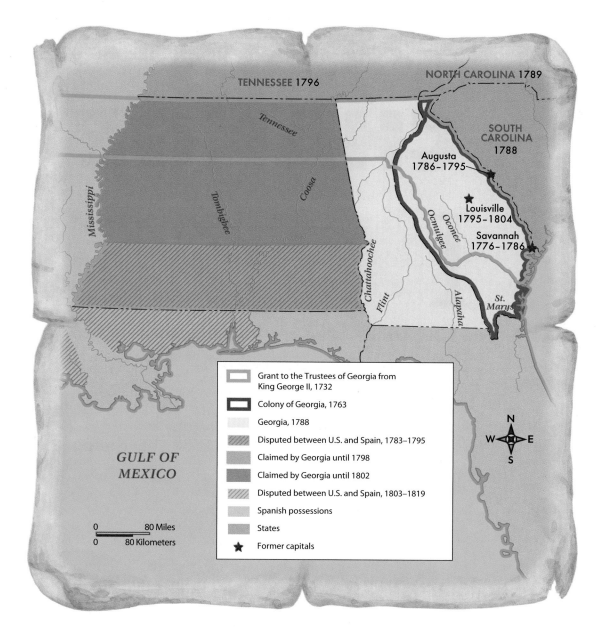

TENNESSEE 1796

NORTH CAROLINA 1789

SOUTH CAROLINA 1788

Tennessee

Coosa

Mississippi

Tombigbee

Augusta
1786–1795

Louisville
1795–1804

Savannah
1776–1786

Chattahoochee

Flint

Oconee

Ocmulgee

Alapaha

St. Marys

GULF OF
MEXICO

☐	Grant to the Trustees of Georgia from King George II, 1732
☐	Colony of Georgia, 1763
	Georgia, 1788
	Disputed between U.S. and Spain, 1783–1795
	Claimed by Georgia until 1798
	Claimed by Georgia until 1802
	Disputed between U.S. and Spain, 1803–1819
	Spanish possessions
	States
★	Former capitals

N
W   E
S

0   80 Miles
0   80 Kilometers

Eli Whitney's cotton gin mechanized the process of removing seeds from cotton, but harvesting it had to be done by hand.

KING COTTON

During the American Revolution, many wealthy Georgians returned to England. After the American victory, some of Georgia's rich rice planters moved to Jamaica and other British-controlled islands in the Caribbean Sea. Homes, farms, and businesses that had been damaged during the war needed to be rebuilt.

To revive the economy and encourage people to settle in Georgia, the state granted free land to war veterans. Cheap land in Georgia also attracted settlers from other states and Europe. Newcomers poured into Savannah and Augusta. Roads were cut into the dense forests, and small towns sprang up in the backcountry.

Georgia became a magnet for New Englanders seeking jobs and business opportunities. Eli Whitney arrived in Georgia from Connecticut in 1793. He visited a cotton plantation near Savannah and watched workers remove seeds from cotton fibers. Cotton grew easily in Georgia, but it was hard to make a profit growing it, because removing the seeds took so long. Whitney's visit inspired him to figure out a better way to clean cotton. He tinkered around and built a simple machine that removed the seeds. His

WORD TO KNOW

bales *large bundles tied together tightly for shipping or storage*

A FORMER SLAVE REMEMBERS

How did Susie King Taylor learn to read as an enslaved young girl, when the laws of Georgia made teaching slaves illegal? Her grandmother in Savannah sent her and her brother to a woman named Mrs. Woodhouse. Susie later wrote about her experience:

She was a free [black] woman and lived on Bay Lane. . . . We went every day about nine o'clock, with our books wrapped in paper to prevent the police or white persons from seeing them. We went in, one at a time, through the gate, into the yard to the kitchen, which was the schoolroom. She had 25 or 30 children whom she taught, assisted by her daughter, Mary Jane. The neighbors would see us going in sometimes, but they supposed we were there learning trades, as it was the custom to give children a trade of some kind. After school we left the same way we entered, one by one.

machine, called a gin (short for "engine"), was a wooden box that used rollers and metal teeth to pull cotton fibers through a metal screen. The seeds were too big to fit through the holes in the screens, so they fell out.

Whitney's cotton gin could clean 50 pounds (23 kg) of cotton a day. Suddenly, cotton production was highly profitable. Cotton soon became Georgia's most important crop. In 1791, Georgia's cotton growers produced only 1,000 **bales** of cotton a year. Within 10 years, they produced 20,000 bales a year. By the mid-1820s, Georgia was the world's largest cotton grower, producing 150,000 bales a year.

To produce all this cotton, many workers were needed to grow, pick, process, and bale cotton. Cotton led to the huge expansion of slavery in Georgia. The state's plantation owners and farmers began importing enslaved people from Africa in record numbers. A large plantation was much like a village, producing almost everything it needed. The planter's family lived in a large mansion and enjoyed all the comforts of the era. The enslaved people, on the other hand, lived in shacks, wore tattered clothing, and endured harsh, and sometimes violent, treatment.

GEORGIA AND THE SLAVE TRADE

Georgia's major port city, Savannah, was the heart of its slave trade. From 1750 to 1766, most enslaved people had come to Georgia from South Carolina or the British colonies in the Caribbean. Starting in 1776, Savannah's slave traders began importing slaves directly from Africa. Most of the enslaved people came from the coast of West Africa. Georgia's rice planters prized enslaved people from this area because it, too, was a rice-growing region. People from West Africa knew how to farm and care for rice.

Papers documented the sale of a slave, such as the one here from 1859.

The trip across the Atlantic took four to six months. When they arrived in Georgia, the enslaved people were confined on Tybee Island to see if they were suffering from any serious diseases. They were then brought to the slave markets of Savannah and sold to planters and farmers to serve as fieldworkers, blacksmiths, cooks, house servants, mechanics, managers, nursemaids, weavers, carpenters, tanners, and jockeys.

In 1798, the Georgia legislature banned importing enslaved people from Africa. Congress passed a national law banning the international slave trade in 1808. Although enslaved people could no longer be brought into the country legally, slave trading within the country was still legal. Illegal slave trading also took place. Georgia's last known slave shipment from Africa occurred in 1858, when a slave ship illegally landed on St. Simons Island carrying more than 400 enslaved Africans.

FAQ

Q: HOW MUCH DID A SLAVE COST?

A: In 1860, Georgia planters would pay as much as $1,800 for a healthy field slave. That's about $44,000 today.

Dockworkers load bales of cotton onto ships in Savannah in 1864.

THE COTTON ECONOMY

By the 1830s, cotton farming dominated the state. Wagon trails soon linked cotton plantations to river docks. Boats transported cotton down Georgia's rivers to cotton markets in Savannah and Brunswick. The invention of the steamboat sped up these deliveries and helped expand the settlement of Georgia. In 1833, the state's first railroad tracks were laid. By 1860, railroad tracks crisscrossed the state.

Boomtowns sprang up in successful cotton-producing areas. One of these towns, Terminus, was located at the end of the Western and Atlantic Railroad, which started in Chattanooga, Tennessee. The town soon became the hub of railroad traffic in Georgia and the entire South. In 1845, Terminus changed its name to Atlanta.

THE TRAIL OF TEARS

The cotton boom had a devastating impact on Native Americans in Georgia. Cotton fever motivated many Georgians, rich and poor, to try to seize as much land as they could. But Creeks and Cherokees owned much of inland Georgia. White Georgians and Native Americans fought over the land. In 1813, a group of Creeks known as the Red Sticks battled with a group of whites who had seized American Indian lands. Another group of Creeks, who were known as the White Sticks, wanted to find a peaceful solution.

The disagreement between the two sides erupted into the Creek War (1813–1814). After about 1,000 Red Sticks overran Fort Mims in Alabama, killing about 400 settlers, the United States entered the war. At the battle at Horseshoe Bend in Alabama, General Andrew Jackson's troops killed about 800 Red Stick warriors. The Red Sticks' leader, Red Eagle, surrendered to Jackson and signed a treaty that gave 23 million acres (8 million ha) of Creek land to the United States. This parcel included the land of the peaceful White Sticks, who opposed Red Eagle and didn't sign the treaty.

Cherokees had a good relationship with the whites and had adopted many of their farming and business methods. In 1827, they formed the Cherokee Nation, wrote a constitution, established a legislature, and elected a principal chief. The Cherokee Nation had a capital city, New Echota, in northern Georgia.

The discovery of gold near Dahlonega, Georgia, proved a disaster for Cherokees. It led government officials and white Americans to demand that Cherokees, Creeks, and other American Indians be removed from the southern United States. In 1830, President Andrew Jackson signed the Indian Removal Act, which required

JOHN ROSS: CHEROKEE LEADER

Under the leadership of John Ross (1790–1866), Cherokees established their own constitutional government. In 1828, he was elected the Cherokees' first principal chief. He fought the Indian Removal Act and headed delegations that argued against the government's plan. One group of Cherokees, however, decided to accept the Removal Act. They signed a treaty with the United States, agreeing to relocation terms for all Cherokees, even those opposed to removal. During the forced relocation of Cherokees to what is now Oklahoma, Ross's wife died of exposure.

 Want to know more? Visit www.factsfornow .scholastic.com and enter the keyword **Georgia**.

eastern Native American nations to move to Indian Territory, land in present-day Oklahoma that had been set aside for Native Americans. Cherokees fought the law, taking their case all the way to the U.S. Supreme Court. The Court refused to recognize the rights of Cherokees.

Georgia began forcing Cherokees to sell their lands. U.S. soldiers placed families in prison camps and then forced them to walk to the new territory west of the Mississippi River. The first forced journey began in the spring of 1838. Another group left in the fall. Nearly 4,000 of the 18,000 Cherokees died during the 800-mile (1,300 km) forced march, mostly from disease, starvation, or exposure to the elements. Cherokees call this journey the Trail of Tears.

Cherokees forced to leave their homes on the Trail of Tears

THE CRAFTS: ESCAPING SLAVERY

William and Ellen Craft (1824–1900; 1826–1891) were slaves who lived in Macon, Georgia. Soon after their marriage in 1848, they made a daring escape from slavery. Ellen was the daughter of an enslaved woman and her white master. She had very light skin. She disguised herself as a Southern gentleman, and William posed as her servant. Together, they made their way to Pennsylvania—and freedom—by train and ship. They continued on to Boston, Massachusetts, joining the large free black community there. Their escape received much coverage in newspapers. They later moved to England. In 1870, they returned to Georgia, buying 1,800 acres (730 ha) of farmland near Savannah.

THE CIVIL WAR

Slave labor made the South's booming cotton economy possible. Enslaved people planted, picked, and baled cotton on the large plantations of wealthy planters. Georgia's slave population had grown to more than 460,000 by 1860. On the eve of the Civil War, Georgia had more slaveholders and enslaved people than any state except Virginia.

Most Georgians were not wealthy plantation owners. Some farmers and merchants did own enslaved people, but they usually owned fewer than 10. The 1860 census showed that 60 percent of the state's farmers didn't own a single enslaved person. These farmers worked hard. They raised cattle and other live-stock and grew crops such as corn and cotton on their small farms. Most, however, remained poor. Most children worked on their families' farms. Only the children of the wealthy received any schooling.

Enslaved workers, including children, picked cotton by hand for plantation owners.

Georgia's richest planters made up only a small portion of the population. Because of their wealth, however, they controlled the state's government and commerce. Along with planters and politicians in other Southern states, they were determined to keep the plantation system and slavery in place.

Wealthy planters used their power to turn poor whites against enslaved African Americans. The planters promoted the idea that people of African descent were inferior to whites and that slavery helped civilize them. Most poor whites were easily convinced that they were superior to blacks. Armed with this belief, poor whites in the South would help planters maintain the ruthless slavery system.

In Northern states, people known as **abolitionists** insisted that slavery was wrong. They demanded that the federal government end it. Many influential Southerners began saying that the slave states should **secede** from the United States.

WORDS TO KNOW

abolitionists *people who work to end slavery*

secede *to withdraw from a group or an organization*

Enslaved people on a plantation on Cockspur Island

They thought the Constitution protected slaveowners and that states had rights of their own.

Slavery became the key issue in the 1860 presidential election. Illinois Republican Abraham Lincoln won the election. Many wealthy Georgians believed Lincoln would abolish slavery. On the floor of the U.S. Senate, one of Georgia's senators shouted out, "The Union . . . is dissolved. . . . Georgia is on the warpath!" On January 19, 1861, Georgia's political leaders voted to secede from the United States. Two months later, Georgia joined the Confederate States of America (CSA). By May, 11 Southern states had seceded and joined the CSA. Alexander H. Stephens, a slaveholder from Georgia, was elected vice president of the new country. Speaking for the new Confederate government, Stephens proudly proclaimed that "the great truth [is] that the Negro is not equal to the white man[,] . . . [and] slavery—subordination to the superior race—is his natural condition." Georgian Thomas Cobb wrote the CSA's constitution, which prohibited the legislature from passing any law banning slavery.

Lincoln believed that it was illegal for states to secede, and he was willing to use troops to keep the Union together. The Confederate army captured Fort Sumter in South Carolina in April 1861, starting the Civil War. Many young Georgians too poor to own enslaved people volunteered to fight against Union troops. By the end of the war, more than 120,000 Georgians had served in the Confederate army. Georgia factories made guns, swords, gunpowder, and other military supplies. With its many railroad lines, Atlanta became the CSA's transportation hub.

Union troops quickly seized Fort Pulaski on Georgia's Tybee Island. They shut down the port of Savannah, preventing supplies from reaching Georgia. For two years, Georgia remained distant from most of the fighting. But

SEE IT HERE!

ATLANTA CYCLORAMA

A cyclorama is a large, circular painting, usually depicting historic scenes. Think of it as an early form of IMAX. The Atlanta Cyclorama lets you experience the Battle of Atlanta. A Union general commissioned the painting to celebrate the Union victory. The cyclorama was 50 feet (15 m) tall, 400 feet (122 m) long, and weighed more than 9,000 pounds (4,000 kg) when it was completed in 1886. It has shrunk a little since then, but it's still the world's largest oil painting.

by September 1863, the Union army was on Georgia's doorstep. Union and Confederate troops fought for two days at Chickamauga, in the state's northwest corner. It was the largest battle in Georgia history. By the time the Union army retreated, more than 34,000 soldiers had been killed or wounded.

In 1864, Union general William Tecumseh Sherman received orders to capture Atlanta. Sherman tried to march his troops around the Confederate army led by General Joseph Johnston. The opposing armies confronted each other in a series of skirmishes. By July, Sherman's army had advanced to within 6 miles (9 km) of Atlanta. Union forces inched forward. Their artillery shells began to explode in the city. After 40 days of shelling, Confederate forces retreated, and Sherman's army marched into Atlanta.

This is an artist's vision of Union forces capturing Atlanta in 1864.

After taking Atlanta in 1864, Union soldiers dismantled railroad tracks throughout the city.

On November 15, Union soldiers set fire to many Atlanta factories and buildings that made weapons and supplies for the Confederate army. The flames spread to other buildings. Soon, fire engulfed the entire city. Only a few buildings survived. The next day, Sherman led his army toward Savannah. His 62,000 troops devastated the Georgia countryside, burning factories and houses and ripping up plantations and farmlands. The troops foraged for food, and they freed enslaved people.

Sherman's troops left a path of destruction 60 miles (100 km) wide and 300 miles (500 km) long. Finally, on December 22, the Union army entered Savannah. Sherman sent the news to Lincoln, writing, "I beg to present to you as a Christmas Gift the City of Savannah."

FIGHTING FOR FREEDOM

More than 186,000 black men served in the Union army. They fought in dozens of crucial battles. About 38,000 black soldiers died in the war. Eighteen earned the Congressional Medal of Honor, the highest U.S. military medal for bravery.

Sherman met with Savannah's African American leaders in January 1865. They asked for land as a payment for generations of black slavery. Sherman agreed. Large tracts of farmland along the coast and on the Sea Islands had been abandoned. Sherman ordered the 400,000 acres (162,000 ha) divided into 40-acre estates for former enslaved people. Generals had no power to do such things, and later, President Andrew Johnson returned the tracts to their original white owners. Congress did not overturn his decision.

The Confederate army surrendered in April 1865. Confederate president Jefferson Davis and his cabinet fled Richmond, Virginia, the Confederate capital. Union troops captured him at Irwinsville, Georgia, in May. They also arrested Vice President Stephens at his home in Crawfordville, Georgia.

The war had touched every Georgian. Forty thousand Georgians either were killed in the war or left and never returned. Sherman's

General Sherman in 1864

Sharecroppers on a Georgia plantation in 1906

troops had burned down a major city and left destruction behind. It would take Georgians decades to rebuild and recover.

RECONSTRUCTION BEGINS

With the defeat of the Confederacy, all enslaved people were freed from bondage. African Americans made up 45 percent of Georgia's population of 1.1 million. Some black Georgians used their freedom to move north. Others stayed and started a new life. They had no money, no land, and few possessions. Many ended up working in the same fields as poorly paid laborers for the same plantation owners who had once enslaved them.

Though slaveholders had lost their free source of labor, they still held political power. The Georgia legislature, called the general assembly, soon passed Black Codes. These were laws that denied African Americans **civil rights**,

SHARECROPPING

After the end of the Civil War, jobs were scarce. Neither newly freed black citizens nor poor whites had land to farm. Plantation owners had lots of land, but they no longer had slaves to work for free.

They developed a new system called sharecropping. A landowner provided a sharecropper with a plot of land to farm. The landowner also provided seeds, tools, and other things needed for the sharecropper and his family to survive, including a house and food. These items were called the furnish. The sharecropper would plant the seeds, tend the crops, and harvest them.

After the harvest, the landowner figured out the sharecropper's earnings. The landowner weighed the harvest and determined its total value. He deducted half this amount for the use of his land. He then subtracted the cost of the furnish. Landowners sometimes cheated sharecroppers by assigning a low price to the crops or by overcharging them. Sharecroppers often worked with worn-out soil and faced cycles of bad weather, which also affected the harvest. They often grew only one crop and were vulnerable to drops in price and demand. No matter how hard sharecroppers worked, they rarely received any money. Sharecropping pulled many families, black and white, into permanent debt.

WORD TO KNOW

civil rights *basic human rights that all citizens in a society are entitled to, such as the right to vote*

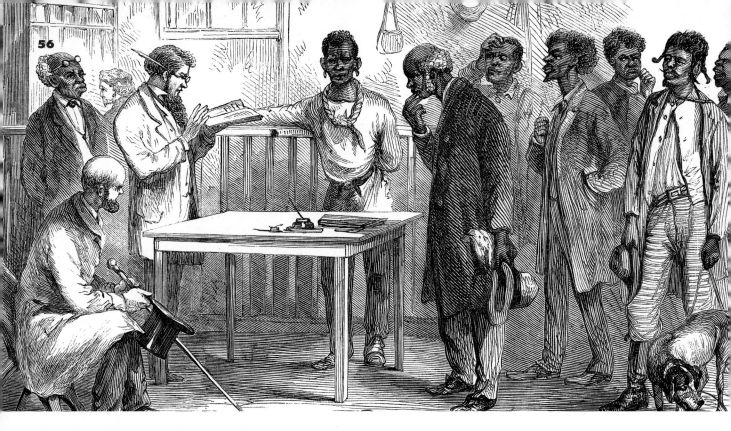

Freed slaves line up to register to vote in
Macon during Reconstruction.

including the right to vote, hold office, serve on juries,
or testify in court against whites. Throughout the
South, former Confederates organized a secret group,
the Ku Klux Klan (KKK), which intimidated African
Americans through violence. Former Confederate general John B. Gordon commanded the KKK in Georgia.

In the first election after the war, Georgia returned
many ex-Confederates to the U.S. Congress and the
Georgia General Assembly. The U.S. Senate refused
to seat Alexander Stephens and Herschel Johnson (a
former Confederate senator). Georgia and nine other
Southern states refused to ratify the 14th Amendment to
the Constitution. This amendment guarantees all citizens
"equal protection of the law," meaning that all citizens
enjoy the same rights, but it also denied some ex-Confederates certain rights. The U.S. Congress responded by
placing these 10 states under military control. This period
is called Reconstruction.

General John Pope governed Georgia for two years. Federal troops enforced his decisions. The federal government also established the Freedmen's Bureau, an agency that helped freed slaves and poor whites throughout the South. The Freedmen's Bureau started reading and writing classes and helped black workers and white landowners agree on fair wages.

In 1867, Congress called on Southern states to write new constitutions that would protect the civil rights of black citizens. The following year, 169 delegates—including

After the Civil War, Georgia struggled to keep its economy stable.

MINI-BIO

SUSIE KING TAYLOR: U.S. ARMY NURSE

Susie King Taylor (1848–1912) was born a slave in Liberty County but was allowed to go to Savannah, where she secretly learned to read and write. One year after the Civil War (1861–1865) started, she and other African Americans fled to an island off Georgia's coast that was occupied by Union soldiers. There she organized a school and taught freed African American students. She later served as a nurse in the Union army, while also teaching black soldiers to read and write during their off-duty hours.

 Want to know more? Visit www.factsfornow .scholastic.com and enter the keyword **Georgia**.

37 black delegates—met to write Georgia's new constitution, which granted civil rights to former enslaved people. But in an election soon after, whites won most of the seats in the Georgia General Assembly. They refused to allow 32 newly elected black legislators to take their seats. In 1870, Georgia elected Jefferson Franklin Long, a former enslaved person and self-educated tailor, to fill a vacancy in the U.S. Congress, but he served only four months. By 1872, former Confederates once again controlled Georgia.

THE NEW SOUTH

Georgia made a slow comeback in the decades after the Civil War. Railroad tracks were repaired. Small textile, flour, and lumber mills sprang up. Coal, limestone, and granite mines opened. Yet times remained hard for most Georgians. Many people barely scratched out a living.

By the early 20th century, Atlanta's economy was booming.

To help improve the sagging economy of Atlanta and the rest of Georgia, Atlanta newspaper editor Henry Grady began a campaign to convince northern companies to open businesses in the state. He coined the phrase "New South" to promote the region. According to Grady, Georgia was full of natural resources and eager workers. He also proclaimed that the state had few racial tensions, which was not true. Still, Grady's efforts paid off. Between 1870 and 1910, Northerners opened many factories and other businesses in Georgia. Atlanta enjoyed an economic revival, which soon spread to other parts of Georgia and other Southern states. Atlanta hosted the World's Fair and International Cotton Exposition in 1881. The event showed off Georgia's agricultural and industrial progress.

Georgia's farmers began growing other crops besides cotton and corn. They planted peach, apple, and pecan trees. These orchards were soon producing lots of fruit. Tobacco, sugarcane, peanuts, and watermelons also became major crops. It was a good thing Georgia's farmers had adopted new crops, because in 1915 the state was infested with boll weevils, beetles that feed on cotton plants. Boll weevils destroyed cotton crops across the state. Georgia's cotton harvest fell by nearly 70 percent. After the United States entered World War I in 1917, Georgia's farmers began to prosper again. The war had created more demand for corn, wheat, tobacco, and other crops.

Atlanta hosted the World's Fair and International Cotton Exposition in 1881.

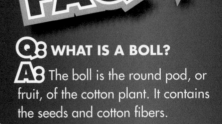

FAQ

Q: WHAT IS A BOLL?
A: The boll is the round pod, or fruit, of the cotton plant. It contains the seeds and cotton fibers.

READ ABOUT

Atlanta, and
other Georgia
cities, prospered
during the Roaring
Twenties.

1941–1945 ▲
*Georgia industries provide
supplies to the U.S. military
during its engagement in
World War II*

1945
*President Franklin
D. Roosevelt dies at
Warm Springs*

1961 ▶
*The first African
American students
are admitted to the
University of Georgia*

CHAPTER FIVE

MORE MODERN TIMES

★

AFTER WORLD WAR I, AMERICAN INDUSTRY BECAME MORE PRODUCTIVE THAN EVER. Companies earned greater profits, and workers earned higher salaries. Many Americans had enough money to buy cars, radios, and telephones. Motion pictures with sound announced the arrival of a modern age. People called these boom years the Roaring Twenties.

◄ **1971**
Jimmy Carter is sworn in as governor

1996 ▲
Atlanta hosts the Summer Olympic Games

2012
The U.S. government authorizes construction of two nuclear reactors in Burke County

Between 1920 and 1925, Georgia's farm population dropped by 370,000.

WORD TO KNOW

stocks *monetary investments in a company*

Franklin Roosevelt shakes hands with a farmer in Georgia while campaigning for president.

GOOD TIMES AND HARD TIMES

Georgia joined in this prosperity. Its major cities expanded as people moved to the city to find work. Georgia's rural areas, however, largely struggled throughout the 1920s. The boll weevils that had arrived in 1915 left much of the land unproductive. Many Georgians abandoned their farms. Some headed to New York, Detroit, Chicago, and other northern cities in search of jobs and city life.

A NEW DEAL

The Roaring Twenties came to an abrupt end when, in October 1929, a panic struck the nation's financial markets. Millions of people rushed to sell their **stocks**, causing stock prices to plunge. Many factories and businesses closed. Others were forced to lay off workers.

By the early 1930s, Georgia, like other states, was in the grip of the Great Depression. Fifteen million of the country's 50 million workers were unemployed. For many, normal life fell apart. Families were shattered or uprooted as people searched for jobs. Soup kitchens fed the hungry and the homeless. Georgia's farmers were hit particularly hard. With so many workers unemployed, few people had enough money to buy meat, vegetables, and other foods. Prices for farm goods plunged, leaving farmers in debt.

President Franklin Roosevelt took office in 1933. He worked to end the Depression with a plan called the New Deal. The New Deal provided relief by creating jobs for unemployed workers. Georgia's governor, Eugene Talmadge, opposed the New Deal relief programs. He was against the federal government getting involved in his state's affairs. He said that Roosevelt's New Deal would destroy Georgia's traditional way of life. But as Georgians saw progress being made under the New Deal in other states, they demanded federal help. Talmadge eventually agreed. Between 1933 and 1940, New Deal programs brought $250 million in assistance to the state. Federally sponsored programs built schools, libraries, public housing projects, and roads. Georgia's farmers were paid to grow less cotton, which helped raise the price of the cotton.

As the years passed, Georgia's businesses and farms slowly recovered from the Depression. More

FAQ

Q: HOW MUCH DID STOCK PRICES FALL AFTER THE 1929 CRASH?

A: Between 1929 and 1933, most stock prices dropped about 80 percent.

MINI-BIO

EUGENE TALMADGE: CONTROVERSIAL GOVERNOR

As the state commissioner of agriculture in the late 1920s, Eugene Talmadge (1884–1946) became highly popular among Georgia's white farmers and rural residents. He was elected governor in 1932, 1934, and 1940. As governor, Talmadge created controversy by opposing the New Deal programs. When he ran for governor once again in 1946, he promised to support racist laws such as those that kept blacks from voting. Talmadge won the election but died before taking office. Even his death caused controversy: three different politicians claimed that they should be the new governor.

? Want to know more? Visit www.factsfornow .scholastic.com and enter the keyword **Georgia**.

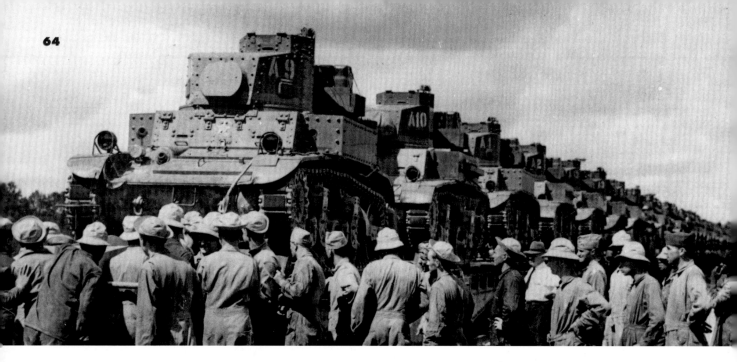

Soldiers at Fort Benning finish loading tanks onto a train bound for Tennessee in 1941.

LIBERTY SHIPS

Liberty ships were cargo boats used in World War II to ferry jeeps, tanks, ammunition, and other supplies to troops in Europe and the Pacific. They were easy to build because the parts were premade. It usually took about 70 days to weld the parts together to make a Liberty ship. Two Georgia shipyards, one in Savannah and one in Brunswick, built 173 Liberty ships. The first ship built in Savannah was named the *James Oglethorpe*, after the founder of the colony of Georgia. Other ships built in the state's shipyards were named after notable Georgians, including Button Gwinnett and Girl Scouts founder Juliette Low.

workers found jobs, and farmers started making money again. A federal program helped bring electricity to rural Georgia. Education, health, and housing programs improved daily life. The state didn't rebound fully, however, until the United States entered World War II in 1941.

A TIME OF WAR

In 1939, after Germany invaded Poland, two of Poland's allies, Britain and France, declared war on Germany. World War II had begun. Germany soon occupied much of western Europe. Meanwhile, Japan had invaded some of its neighbors in Asia. A surprise Japanese attack on Pearl Harbor, a U.S. naval base in Hawai'i, in December 1941 pulled the United States into the war.

The U.S. war effort revived Georgia's economy. Thousands of soldiers trained at Fort Benning, Fort Gordon, and other military bases in the state. Businesses and farmers near these bases helped supply the military's needs. Shipyards in Savannah and Brunswick built cargo ships called Liberty ships. By 1943, Bell Aircraft in Marietta employed 20,000 workers and built bombers for the U.S. Air Force. Between 1941 and 1945, Georgians' income doubled.

As the war in Europe drew to a close, Georgia appeared in news headlines when President Franklin Roosevelt died in Warm Springs on April 12, 1945. He had built a house there in 1932 so he could exercise in the springs' hot water. A crippling disease called polio had robbed Roosevelt of the use of his legs 25 years earlier. After he was elected president, his Warm Springs home became known as the Little White House. Roosevelt had arrived there in late March 1945 in poor health. Less than two weeks later, he died of a stroke.

THE CIVIL RIGHTS MOVEMENT

For a century after the end of slavery, African Americans throughout the South struggled to gain basic civil rights. In 1906, white mobs killed dozens of black people and wounded many others in Atlanta because a newspaper alleged that black men had assaulted white females in the city. The riot showed that the "New South" had in fact changed little where race was concerned. Between 1882 and 1930, mob violence killed more than 3,000 people across the South. In Georgia alone, more than 450 African Americans were **lynched**. Lynching victims were usually accused of crimes against whites. Some of their "crimes" were simply that they were African Americans who were confident or assertive.

Throughout the South, a system of **segregation** known as Jim Crow separated blacks from whites. Black students were not allowed to attend the same schools as white students. Blacks were banned from swimming at public pools and beaches, eating at restaurants, and staying at hotels used by whites. They even had to drink from separate water fountains, sit in separate train cars, and use

FAQ

Q8 WHERE DID THE NAME JIM CROW COME FROM?

A8 Jim Crow was the name of a black character portrayed by white performers in the 1830s. Whites used the singing, dancing, smiling character to ridicule African Americans.

WORDS TO KNOW

lynched *killed by a mob without a lawful trial*

segregation *separation from others, according to race, class, ethnic group, religion, or other factors*

WALTER WHITE: CIVIL RIGHTS LEADER

Walter White (1893–1955) was born into a prominent African American family in Atlanta. He graduated from Atlanta University in 1916. White was light-skinned and could have chosen to live as a white person in the segregated South. As a teenager, however, he had witnessed his family being threatened during the Atlanta race riots of 1906. He vowed to fight racism. White moved to New York in 1917 to work for the National Association for the Advancement of Colored People (NAACP). In 1929, he was selected to head the organization. White led the fight to achieve equality for African American for 26 years.

? Want to know more? Visit www.factsfornow .scholastic.com and enter the keyword **Georgia**.

WORD TO KNOW

boycott *the organized refusal to use a service or buy a product, as a form of protest*

separate restrooms. Georgia's constitution required a person to own property and prove that he had a Confederate ancestor in order to vote. How many African Americans could prove that they had Confederate ancestors? The Georgia Assembly passed other laws to make it impossible for black Georgians to vote. Women of any race could not vote in Georgia until after the approval in 1919 of the 19th Amendment to the U.S. Constitution, which gave all American women the right to vote.

By the mid-1950s, many African Americans were challenging the Jim Crow laws. In *Brown v. Board of Education* (1954), the U.S. Supreme Court ruled that racially segregated schools were unconstitutional. States had to treat all students equally, no matter their race.

In December 1955, Rosa Parks was arrested when she refused to give up her seat on a Montgomery, Alabama, bus to a white passenger. A local 27-year-old pastor, Martin Luther King Jr., led an effort to overturn segregated seating laws on Montgomery's city buses. The Atlanta-born minister organized a **boycott**, and the Supreme Court ruled that a city could not force black people to sit in the back of the bus. King's message of peaceful resistance to segregation propelled him to leadership in the U.S. civil rights movement.

The *Brown* decision and the success of the bus boycott encouraged African Americans throughout the

African Americans demonstrate outside of Albany's city hall.

South to unite against Jim Crow. In 1961, the University of Georgia admitted its first black students. Other colleges and public schools slowly began allowing black students into their classrooms. In Savannah, local black leaders protested segregation in many ways. They organized **sit-ins** at lunch counters, wade-ins at beaches, and boycotts of white businesses. Their efforts finally paid off in 1963, when city leaders agreed to end segregation. Then Macon, Rome, Brunswick, and other cities agreed to desegregate. Protesters in Augusta and other towns,

WORD TO KNOW

sit-ins *acts of protest that involve sitting in racially segregated places and refusing to leave*

MINI-BIO

CHARLAYNE HUNTER-GAULT: A TRAILBLAZER

Charlayne Hunter-Gault (1942–) was one of the first two African American students admitted to the University of Georgia (UGA). In 1961, a federal court ordered UGA to admit Hunter-Gault and another black student, Hamilton Holmes. White students taunted Hunter-Gault, and police had to disperse a mob outside of her room. After graduation, she became a successful journalist. She worked as a reporter for the New York Times, a correspondent for PBS's MacNeil/Lehrer NewsHour, and bureau chief for Atlanta's Cable News Network (CNN).

 Want to know more? Visit www.factsfornow.scholastic.com and enter the keyword **Georgia**.

however, repeatedly encountered violence from white officials and citizens. In rural areas, the struggle against Jim Crow had few successes.

"I HAVE A DREAM"

After the success of the Montgomery bus boycott, Martin Luther King Jr. continued to promote nonviolent resistance. Between 1957 and 1968, he joined hundreds of campaigns for racial justice. He traveled more than 6 million miles (10 million km) and gave more than 2,500 speeches. He helped plan voter registration drives, was often arrested, and became co-pastor with his father at Ebenezer Baptist Church in Atlanta.

In August 1963, King led a historic protest called the March on Washington, D.C. Standing in front of 250,000 people, he delivered his stirring "I Have a Dream" speech. In one part, his powerful voice rang out, "I have a dream that one day on the red hills of Georgia, sons of former slaves and the sons of former slave owners will be able to sit down together at the table of brotherhood." King was awarded the Nobel Peace Prize in 1964, becoming the youngest person to receive the honor.

King's life ended on April 4, 1968, when he was assassinated in Memphis, Tennessee. People around the world mourned his death. King's birthday is now celebrated as a national holiday.

THE END OF SEGREGATION

The long battle against segregation in the South changed the country. The U.S. Congress enacted two laws—the Civil Rights Act of 1964 and the Voting Rights Act of 1965—to guarantee African Americans educational, social, economic, and political

Martin Luther King Jr.

rights. Atlanta soon became known as one of the most progressive cities in the South. In his 1971 inaugural address, Governor Jimmy Carter proclaimed, "I say to you quite frankly that the time for racial discrimination is over." Two years later, attorney Maynard Jackson was the first African American to be elected mayor of Atlanta.

A MODERN STATE

In the 1980s and 1990s, Georgia boomed. In Atlanta, skyscrapers rose up and suburbs doubled in population. By 1990, 40 percent of the state's population lived in the Atlanta area.

Georgia has hosted many important events in recent decades. In 1996, Atlanta hosted the Summer Olympics. Then, in 2004, the G8 Summit, an annual meeting of the leaders of eight powerful nations, was held on the Sea Islands.

In 2012, a federal agency authorized construction of two more nuclear reactors in Burke County. The decision will help Georgia meet its growing energy demands in the years to come.

The closing ceremonies for the 1996 Summer Olympics

READ ABOUT

Atlanta Falcons fans cheer on their team during a January 2013 playoff game.

CHAPTER SIX

PEOPLE

★

WITH ITS LIVELY CAPITAL CITY, PLEASANT CLIMATE, AND STRONG ECONOMY, GEORGIA ATTRACTS MANY NEWCOMERS. Gaining more than 100,000 people per year, Georgia is the fastest-growing state east of the Rocky Mountains. With a population in 2010 of almost 9.7 million people, Georgia is ranked ninth in population among the 50 states.

Big City Life

This list shows the population of Georgia's biggest cities.

Atlanta 420,003
Augusta-Richmond County . . . .
. 195,844
Columbus 189,885
Savannah 136,286
Athens-Clarke County . .115,452

Source: U.S. Census Bureau, 2010 census

Where Georgians Live

The colors on this map indicate population density throughout the state. The darker the color, the more people live there.

LIFE IN GEORGIA

What's life like today in Georgia? It depends on who you are and where you live. About 75 percent of Georgians make their homes in urban areas. The other nearly 25 percent live in rural areas.

Big-city life in Atlanta is bustling. More than 4 million people live in the Atlanta metropolitan area, which includes 28 counties. Wide highways circle the city

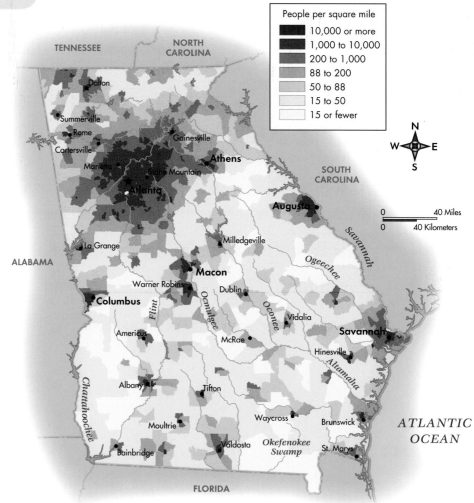

People per square mile
- 10,000 or more
- 1,000 to 10,000
- 200 to 1,000
- 88 to 200
- 50 to 88
- 15 to 50
- 15 or fewer

and shoot out in all directions like spokes on a bicycle wheel. Traffic jams are common, with commuters from the suburbs driving many miles to and from work. In contrast, life in Georgia's other cities is calmer and less hurried. Many Georgians now live in the suburbs. Other Georgians live in small towns with historic downtowns.

Most of Georgia's rural areas are doing well. Its rural population increased almost 15 percent between 1990 and 2000, though the rate of increase slowed after 2000. About 47,000 family farms operate in Georgia.

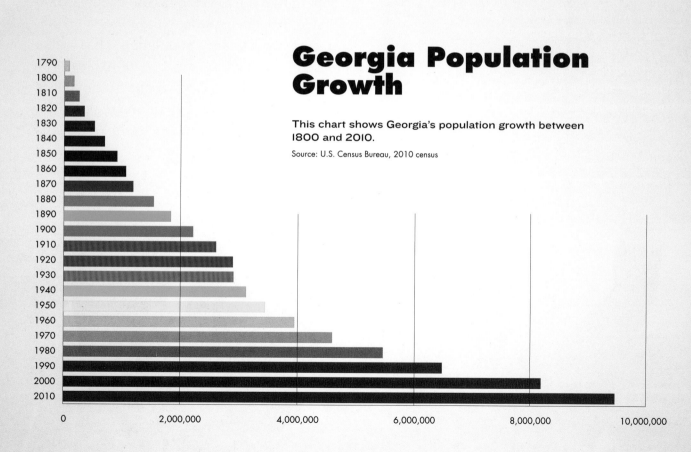

Georgia Population Growth

This chart shows Georgia's population growth between 1800 and 2010.

Source: U.S. Census Bureau, 2010 census

A UNIQUE CULTURE

The Sea Islands region of Georgia is home to a people called the Geechee (they are known as the Gullah in South Carolina's Sea Islands). The Geechee are descendants of West Africans who were enslaved and brought to North America to grow rice. They began arriving on the Sea Islands in 1750, when slavery became legal in Georgia.

The enslaved people on the Sea Islands held on to the cultures and traditions of their homelands. Because of the islands' isolation, Geechee customs developed with little influence from mainland Georgia. Geechee language is a combination of words from various West African languages and words borrowed from English. One distinctive Geechee tradition is the ring shout. At religious meetings, worshippers clap their hands in rhythm while singing spiritual songs and moving in a circle. The Geechee have preserved a rich heritage that spans two continents and more than two centuries.

A DIVERSE PEOPLE

Georgia has a rich ethnic makeup, including citizens of African, European, Asian, and American Indian descent. Today, roughly 3.1 million African Americans live in Georgia. If the current rate of growth continues, Georgia will soon have the nation's largest black population, surpassing Texas, Florida, and New York.

Hispanics, people who trace their roots to Spanish-speaking countries, are the fastest-growing ethnic group in Georgia. The number of Hispanics living in Georgia rose from 435,000 in 2000 to 850,000 in 2010.

Georgia's Asian population has also increased considerably since 2000. Asians now make up more about 3.2 percent of the state's population. Most Asians live in one region—the Atlanta area. About three-quarters of Asians

The Geechee-Gullah Ring Shouters perform at an outdoor ceremony.

living in Georgia trace their heritage to India, China, Vietnam, and Korea.

Few Native Americans live in Georgia today. In 2012, Native Americans made up only 0.2 percent of Georgia's population. Members of many different groups live in the state, but people of Cherokee or Creek heritage are the most numerous.

In 2011, the Georgia legislature passed a new immigration law to crack down on people living in the United States illegally. The law allows police to question people suspected of having committed crimes about their immigration status. The law also sets harsher penalties for anyone who hires an illegal immigrant.

MINI-BIO

LEAH WARD SEARS: CHIEF JUSTICE

Leah Ward Sears (1955–) served as the chief justice of the Georgia Supreme Court from 2005 to 2009. In 1992, she was appointed by Georgia governor Zell Miller to become the first woman and the youngest judge to sit on the Supreme Court of Georgia. Sears was born in Germany and moved throughout the world because her father was an army colonel. She graduated from the law school at Emory University in Atlanta in 1980. She currently works as a lawyer in a private law firm.

? **Want to know more?** Visit www.factsfornow .scholastic.com and enter the keyword **Georgia**.

People QuickFacts

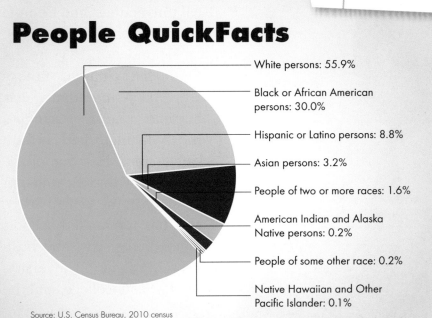

- White persons: 55.9%
- Black or African American persons: 30.0%
- Hispanic or Latino persons: 8.8%
- Asian persons: 3.2%
- People of two or more races: 1.6%
- American Indian and Alaska Native persons: 0.2%
- People of some other race: 0.2%
- Native Hawaiian and Other Pacific Islander: 0.1%

Source: U.S. Census Bureau, 2010 census

Georgia has 159 counties. The only state with more counties is Texas, which has 254, but it is four times bigger than the Peach State!

SCHOOL DAYS

Georgia's first government-supported high school opened in Augusta, the state capital at the time, in 1783. Although several other cities also established schools, the state government did little to fund education until after the Civil War. Georgia adopted a nine-month school year in 1949. Until then, many schools held classes for only four months a year, to allow children to help out on their family farms. Despite the Supreme Court's 1955 ruling striking down segregated schools, most Georgia schools remained segregated until the early 1970s.

Georgia has a long history of higher education. In 1785, the general assembly agreed to establish a public university. Sixteen years later, students attended the first classes at the University of Georgia in Athens. Today, the university is a major research and teaching institution and is part of the University System of Georgia, which oversees 33 colleges and universities, including Georgia Institute of Technology (Georgia Tech), one of the nation's top technological universities, and Georgia State University.

Georgia's public schools serve a diverse population.

Founded in 1836 by the Methodist Church, Emory University in Atlanta has become one of Georgia's most distinguished private universities. It is one of the fastest-growing research universities in the United States and has top-ranked schools of medicine, law, and business. Mercer University, Agnes Scott College, and the

Campus of Emory University

Savannah College of Art and Design are other notable private colleges and universities in Georgia.

Georgia is also home to 10 historically black colleges and universities. These institutions were founded before most of Georgia's colleges accepted African American students. Today, they educate students of all races. Atlanta's Morehouse College is an all-male college, one of only five in the United States. Civil rights leader Martin Luther King Jr., former U.S. surgeon general David Satcher, and film director Spike Lee graduated from Morehouse. Spelman College, a women's college in Atlanta, and Clark Atlanta University are two other notable historically black colleges in the state.

HOW TO TALK LIKE A GEORGIAN

Take a cue from the locals and call Atlanta "A-town" and the Chattahoochee River "the Hooch." If you order "greens" in a Georgia restaurant, you probably won't be getting salad greens. Most likely, you'll be served stewed collard, mustard, or turnip greens. And if you order tea, it will be southern-style: very sweet and served with lots of ice.

HOW TO EAT LIKE A GEORGIAN

When you think of Georgia foods, what probably comes to mind are the state's two most famous ones—peaches and peanuts. But you'll find lots of other yummy eats throughout the state. Seafood and rice dishes are a specialty on the Sea Islands and along the coast. Food of African American origin, sometimes called soul food, is popular. Soul food dishes include fried chicken, black-eyed peas, fried okra, chitterlings (hog intestines), and collard greens. To wash it down, grab a Coca-Cola, the world-famous soft drink invented in Atlanta.

A restaurant's roadside sign advertises barbeque.

MENU

WHAT'S ON THE MENU IN GEORGIA?

★ ★ ★

Grits

Boiled peanuts

This popular snack—freshly harvested peanuts boiled for hours in salty water—is available during peanut season (May to November).

Grits

Grits are small, broken-up grains of corn that are cooked in water to make porridge. They are usually eaten at breakfast but are some-times served at other meals.

Peach pie

You know that Georgia is the Peach State, and you know what a pie is. So you shouldn't be surprised that Georgians eat a lot of peach pie. (And pecan pie, too!)

Peach pie

TRY THIS RECIPE
Brunswick Stew

There are about as many Brunswick stew recipes as there are cooks in Georgia. Some people use chicken, pork, or beef—or all three—as the meat. Here's one version to try. (Be sure to have a grown-up nearby to help.)

Ingredients:
1 tablespoon vegetable oil
1 pound meat, cut into chunks (chicken, pork, or beef; or leave it out for a vegetarian stew)
1 large onion, chopped
1 celery rib, chopped
1 green pepper, seeded and chopped
1 16-ounce can diced tomatoes
2 medium potatoes, peeled and cubed
2 small hot peppers, seeded and sliced
½ teaspoon dried thyme
½ teaspoon dried basil
Water
Salt and pepper, to taste

Instructions:
1. Add the oil to a large pot over medium-high heat. Brown the meat, transfer to a bowl, and set it aside.
2. Add the onion, celery, and green pepper to the unwashed pot and cook until softened.
3. Add the tomatoes (with juice), potatoes, hot peppers, thyme, and basil. Add the browned meat and enough water to cover the ingredients by about 1 inch. Bring to a boil, then cover and cook on low heat for about 90 minutes.
4. Add the corn, lima beans, and okra. Cook uncovered for about 60 minutes, stirring often. Add salt and pepper to taste. Makes 8 servings.

MASTER QUILTER

One of the best-known African American quilt makers, Harriet Powers (1837–1910) was born into slavery near Athens. Little is known about her life until 1886. That year, she displayed one of her quilts at a fair in Athens. The quilt (below) depicts biblical stories in 11 panels. An art teacher offered to buy the quilt, but Powers wouldn't sell it. Five years later, however, she agreed to sell the quilt to the art teacher for $5. The buyer wrote down Powers's description of each panel's meaning. Only one other quilt made by Powers survives today.

THE ARTS

Georgia has produced a wide variety of writers. In his Uncle Remus tales, Joel Chandler Harris preserved many of the **folktales** of Georgia's African American community that he had heard as a young adult.

In the 20th century, many Georgia writers made a name for themselves. Erskine Caldwell's best-selling novels *Tobacco Road* and *God's Little Acre* deal with the lives of sharecroppers in rural Georgia. Black fiction writers, including Jean Toomer, Georgia Douglas Johnson, and Frank Yerby, wrote about the difficulties that African Americans faced in the segregated South.

Atlanta's Margaret Mitchell won the Pulitzer Prize for *Gone with the Wind*, her 1936 novel set in Georgia during the Civil War and Reconstruction. *Gone with the Wind* was the best-selling American novel of the 20th century and became a blockbuster movie.

Georgia also has a firm place in the art world. The works of Lucy May Stanton, Lamar Dodd, and Howard Finster are well known, and Atlanta's High Museum of Art is perhaps the premier art museum in the South.

Georgia has produced many talented musicians. Augusta native Jessye Norman is one of the world's finest sopranos. In the 20th century, jazz fans thrilled to the sounds of Fletcher Henderson, Lena Horne, and Johnny Mercer. The blues rose out of southern African American communities. Early blues greats from Georgia include Ma Rainey, Blind Willie McTell, and Tampa Red Whitaker. Ray Charles, James Brown, Gladys Knight, Toni Braxton, and Usher are just a few of the big rhythm-and-blues stars from the Peach State.

Georgia is also well represented in pop music, with stars as diverse as Little Richard, Ludacris, the B-52s, OutKast, and REM all coming out of the state.

Singer Ray Charles made a best-selling recording of "Georgia on My Mind," which became the state song in 1979.

Today, Georgia has a thriving film industry. The state has become a popular location for an increasing number of films, commercials, TV shows, and music videos. The state's diverse geography, mild climate, and transportation network have made it an attractive choice for film companies. To help grow the industry, the state government has passed laws that give film-makers tax breaks to film in Georgia. More than 800 companies that offer film equipment and skilled film workers operate in the state.

SPORTS

Atlanta is a big sports town. Its major league baseball team, the Braves, won the Eastern Division of the National League 14 times in a row (1991–2005). During that stretch, the team won the National League pennant five times and the World Series once (1995). The Atlanta Falcons battle other teams in the National Football League (NFL). The Falcons made it all the

SEE IT HERE!

FINSTER'S PARADISE GARDEN

A self-taught artist, Howard Finster (c. 1915–2001) created thousands of paintings, sculptures, drawings, and prints. His work has appeared in museums around the world. Born in Alabama, he moved to Chattooga County, Georgia, in 1937. In 1961, he began filling the area behind his Pennville home with a jumble of sculptures, towers made of bicycle parts, and other found objects. He called it Plant Farm Museum and later renamed it Paradise Garden. Visitors are welcome to take a tour.

Fans fill Turner Field in Atlanta to watch the Braves.

MINI-BIO

JACKIE ROBINSON: BREAKING BASEBALL'S COLOR BARRIER

Jackie Robinson (1919–1972), born near Cairo, Georgia, was the first African American to play major league baseball in the 20th century. On April 15, 1947, he broke baseball's color barrier when he started at first base for the Brooklyn Dodgers. He soon began playing second base. Robinson was the first black player to be named Rookie of the Year, to win a Most Valuable Player award, and to be inducted into the National Baseball Hall of Fame. He was widely admired for maintaining his cool while being showered with racial slurs by the crowd and by opposing players. He paved the way for later black baseball players.

 Want to know more? Visit www.factsfornow .scholastic.com and enter the keyword **Georgia**.

way to the NFL's championship game, the Super Bowl, in 1998. The Atlanta Hawks hoop it up with other National Basketball Association (NBA) teams. The Hawks have had several Hall of Famers, including "Pistol" Pete Maravich and Dominique Wilkins. Atlanta was also home to the Thrashers, a National Hockey League team from 1999 until 2011.

College sports are wildly popular in Georgia. The Bulldogs of the University of Georgia in Athens are traditional powers in football, baseball, tennis, and gymnastics. The

Yellow Jackets of Georgia Tech field strong teams in football, basketball, baseball, and tennis.

The Georgia Sports Hall of Fame celebrates outstanding athletes who were born in, played in, or lived in Georgia. Included are football legend Jim Brown; baseball greats Ty Cobb, Jackie Robinson, and Hank Aaron; golf superstars Bobby Jones and Nancy Lopez; and boxing champion Evander Holyfield.

University of Georgia Bulldogs quarterback Matthew Stafford prepares to pass in a 2007 game against Mississippi.

READ ABOUT

Members of the state legislature applaud General James Oglethorpe and other costumed participants in the Georgia Day festivities.

CHAPTER SEVEN

GOVERNMENT

★

LIKE MANY STATES, GEORGIA HAS HAD MORE THAN ONE CONSTITUTION OVER THE YEARS. In fact, Georgia has had 10 different constitutions! The first was adopted in 1777 when Georgians were fighting for independence from Great Britain. New constitutions were also written when Georgia first joined the United States, when it joined the Confederate States of America, and when it rejoined the United States after the Civil War.

Capitol Facts

Here are some fascinating facts about Georgia's state capitol.

Exterior height	272 feet (33 m)
Number of stories high	4
Length	348 feet (106 m)
Surrounding park	5 acres (2 ha)
Construction dates	1884–1889
Cost of construction	$998,157

Georgia's voters approved the most recent constitution in 1983. The new constitution is much shorter than earlier ones—about half the size of the document it replaced—and is written in plain English rather than legal language. It keeps many elements from Georgia's earlier constitutions. For example, it still divides the state government into three branches: the legislative, the executive, and the judicial. The new constitution also made changes, such as requiring that judges be elected rather than appointed.

THE STATE CAPITOL

Georgia's capitol is located in downtown Atlanta. Built in the Renaissance style (think Michelangelo), it opened in 1889. It was the city's tallest structure at the time. A distinctive dome, covered with a thin layer

A gold dome tops Georgia's state capitol.

of gold, was added in 1957. The gold, which was donated by citizens, is from the Dahlonega gold mines in northern Georgia. The capitol houses the offices of the governor and other state officials, the Georgia Supreme Court, the state library, and the chambers of the Georgia General Assembly.

Georgia's Capital

This map shows places of interest in Atlanta, Georgia's capital city.

JULIAN BOND: A VOICE FOR EQUALITY

When Julian Bond (1940–) retired from the Georgia senate, he had been elected to public office more times than any other black Georgian. As a student at Atlanta's Morehouse College in the early 1960s, he became a key figure in the civil rights movement. He was active in voter registration drives—efforts to sign up black voters, many of whom had been prevented from voting before—and in protests against segregation. Bond continued to champion equality for all Americans during his 20 years (1967–1986) as a legislator. He was awarded the National Freedom Medal in 2002.

Want to know more? Visit www.factsfornow.scholastic.com and enter the keyword **Georgia**.

THE LEGISLATIVE BRANCH

Georgia's legislative branch is called the general assembly. Its job is to make new laws, change or get rid of old laws, consider proposed changes to the state constitution, and help the governor prepare the state budget. The general assembly consists of two chambers. The senate has 56 members, and the house of representatives has 180 members. Its total of 236 members makes it one of the largest state legislatures in the country. Georgia's voters elect their senators and representatives for two-year terms.

Georgians have other ways besides voting to influence what laws are passed. In 2003, Carterville's Alan and LuGina Brown lost their 17-year-old son, Joshua. He died in a one-car accident that may have been preventable. Wanting to prevent similar tragedies, they worked closely with their state senator to propose a law encouraging and funding better driver education

Georgia's house of representatives and senate in session

for Georgia teens. Eighty-seven percent of the Georgia General Assembly voted in favor of the bill. Known as Joshua's Law, the teen drivers' law went into effect on January 1, 2007.

THE EXECUTIVE BRANCH

The governor heads Georgia's executive branch. Voters elect the governor to a four-year term. No governor can serve more than two terms in a row. The governor has the power to **veto** bills passed by the legislature. The legislature, however, can overturn the veto with a two-thirds vote.

SEE IT HERE!

GOVERNOR'S MANSION

The governor's mansion is located in northeastern Atlanta. Built in 1967 in the Greek Revival style, it is the official home of the governor. The mansion has three stories and 30 rooms. On tours of the mansion, you will see Federal-era (think George Washington) furniture and paintings by Georgia artists.

WORD TO KNOW

veto *to reject a proposed piece of legislation*

MINI-BIO

JAMES EARL (JIMMY) CARTER: A GEORGIAN IN THE WHITE HOUSE

In 1974, after four years as Georgia's governor, Jimmy Carter (1924—) announced that he was running for president. Carter was little known outside his own state, but he won the 1976 presidential election. He is the first, and so far the only, Georgian to serve as president. As president, Carter was responsible for bringing together Egypt's president Anwar el-Sadat and Israel's prime minister Menachem Begin for peace talks. But then, in 1979, a group of Iranian students seized 66 American hostages in Iran. Carter was defeated when he ran for a second term as president in 1980. Since leaving office, Carter has remained busy, working with Habitat for Humanity, an organization of volunteers who build free homes for low-income families. He also established the Carter Center in Atlanta to champion human rights. Carter was awarded the Nobel Peace Prize in 2002 for his tireless work for human rights. He was born, and still lives, in Plains.

? Want to know more? Visit www.factsfornow .scholastic.com and enter the keyword **Georgia**.

MINI-BIO

STACEY ABRAMS: HOUSE MINORITY LEADER

Democrat Stacey Abrams (1973–) is the house minority leader of the Georgia General Assembly. She is the first woman to lead either political party in the assembly and the first African American to lead a party in the Georgia House of Representatives. Born in Wisconsin, she studied public affairs at the University of Texas and received a degree in law from Yale University. She was selected one of the "100 Most Influential Georgians" by Georgia Trend magazine in 2012 and 2013.

 Want to know more? Visit www.factsfornow .scholastic.com and enter the keyword **Georgia**.

The governor has a big job. He or she directs how the state's budget is spent and oversees the work of more than 145,000 state employees who administer state laws and provide many services to Georgians and visitors. Governors have to deal with whatever problems arise in the state. When deadly tornadoes swept through Georgia in April 2011, Governor Nathan Deal requested federal funds to pay for efforts to rebuild the devastated areas. By August, the state had received $4.7 million from the federal government.

Firefighters battle a wildfire near Waycross in April 2007.

Representing Georgians

This list shows the number of elected officials who represent Georgia, both on the state and national levels.

OFFICE	NUMBER	LENGTH OF TERM
State senators	56	2 years
State representatives	180	2 years
U.S. senators	2	6 years
U.S. representatives	13	2 years
Presidential electors	15	—

Georgia's State Government

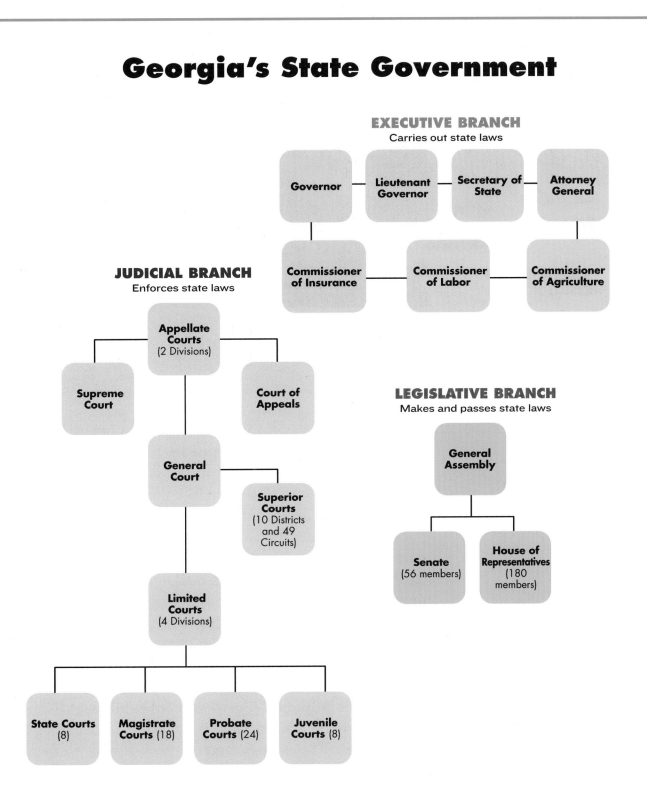

EXECUTIVE BRANCH
Carries out state laws

Governor — Lieutenant Governor — Secretary of State — Attorney General

Commissioner of Insurance — Commissioner of Labor — Commissioner of Agriculture

JUDICIAL BRANCH
Enforces state laws

Appellate Courts (2 Divisions)

Supreme Court — Court of Appeals

General Court — Superior Courts (10 Districts and 49 Circuits)

Limited Courts (4 Divisions)

State Courts (8) — Magistrate Courts (18) — Probate Courts (24) — Juvenile Courts (8)

LEGISLATIVE BRANCH
Makes and passes state laws

General Assembly

Senate (56 members) — House of Representatives (180 members)

A prosecutor stands while addressing the court during a hearing in Atlanta.

WORD TO KNOW

appeals *legal proceedings in which a court is asked to change the decision of a lower court*

THE JUDICIAL BRANCH

The judicial branch has three levels of courts: superior courts, appeals court, and the Georgia Supreme Court. Trial court judges oversee criminal and civil cases in superior courts. Voters elect superior court justices.

The Georgia Court of **Appeals** has 12 members, who are elected to two-year terms. This court hears appeals of decisions made in trial courts.

The highest court in the state, the Georgia Supreme Court reviews decisions made by lower courts. For example, in February 2013, the supreme court ruled on the case of Bobby Buckner. Buckner was accused of murder in 2007 but not brought to trial for more than four years. The trial court ruled that his constitutional right to a speedy trial had been denied and dismissed the case. The state appealed the court's decision, but the supreme court upheld the trial judge's original decision. The supreme court also handles all cases that question whether a state law is valid under Georgia's constitution. The state's voters elect the supreme court's seven justices to six-year terms.

Georgia's Counties

This map shows the 159 counties in Georgia. Atlanta, the state capital, is indicated with a star.

1. DEKALB
2. CLAYTON
3. FAYETTE
4. SPALDING
5. BUTTS
6. NEWTON
7. ROCKDALE
8. OCONEE
9. CLARKE
10. OGLETHORPE
11. FRANKLIN
12. HABERSHAM
13. GLASCOCK
14. CHATTAHOOCHEE
15. MONTGOMERY

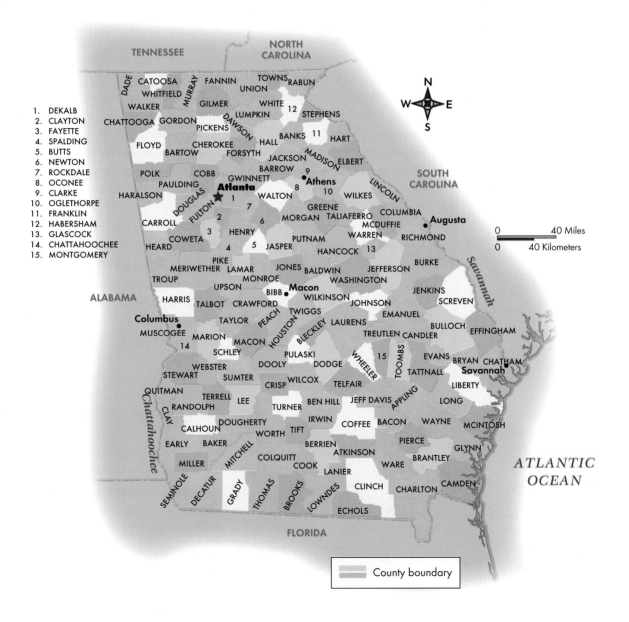

THINK ABOUT IT!

Rattlesnake Roundups

Some Georgians live in areas where venomous rattlesnakes also live. Since 1960, several Georgia communities have held rattlesnake roundups. In a roundup, hunters catch and kill as many as 1,000 eastern diamondback and timber rattlesnakes. The events' organizers point out that roundups lower the number of snakes that are a threat to humans, farm animals, and pets. The roundups also feature parades and other festivities that attract thousands of people and raise money for charities. Organizers also stress that the snakes are milked for venom, which can be used to make antivenin, a medicine for snakebites. One organizer explained, "That's the whole reason we have it."

Environmentalists and others note that other animals, such as tortoises and gophers, are sometimes harmed or killed during the roundups. They also believe that the roundups endanger rattlesnake populations, are inhumane, and encourage disrespect for wildlife and the environment. And, as a spokesperson for the Humane Society of the United States pointed out, "no U.S. producer of antivenin would knowingly purchase venom collected at roundups."

Source: *Savannah Morning News,* March 6, 2007

LOCAL RULE

In addition to the state government, Georgia also has governments at the county and city levels. In Georgia, counties are the political center for most citizens. Counties oversee elections, maintain roads, and administer public assistance programs. Under the state constitution, counties can provide police and fire protection, garbage disposal, recreational facilities, and public housing and transportation. In most counties, commissioners are in charge of running the government. A city council and a mayor typically oversee city governments.

Counties are responsible for providing police protection to their residents.

MINI-BIO

SHIRLEY FRANKLIN: ATLANTA MAYOR

Shirley Franklin (1945–) was elected mayor of Atlanta in 2001. She was the first woman to serve as the city's mayor. Franklin was the first female African American mayor of a major city in the South and the fourth black mayor of Atlanta. Born in Pennsylvania, she earned her bachelor's degree from Howard University and a master's degree from the University of Pennsylvania. Before being elected mayor, Franklin worked in the administrations of former Atlanta mayors Maynard Jackson and Andrew Young.

? **Want to know more?** Visit www.factsfornow .scholastic.com and enter the keyword **Georgia**.

State Flag

Georgia's state flag consists of three horizontal stripes of red, white, and red, with a blue square in the upper left corner. Centered in the square is the state coat of arms, in gold, with the phrase "In God We Trust." Thirteen white stars, symbolizing Georgia and the 12 other original states that formed the United States, circle the coat of arms.

This flag was adopted on May 8, 2003, becoming the state's third flag in a 27-month period, a national record. It replaced a flag that had been adopted in January 2001 to replace the 1956 flag. The flag from the 1950s was controversial because it featured a large version of the Confederate battle flag, which many people consider a symbol of racism. The 2001 flag depicted a smaller version of the battle flag, along with other flags that had flown over Georgia. The adoption of the 2001 flag did not end the controversy, which resulted in the 2003 redesign.

State Seal

The front of the Great Seal of Georgia depicts three pillars supporting an arch. The pillars symbolize the three branches of government. Each has a scroll inscribed with a single word that together form the state motto: Wisdom, Justice, and Moderation. A uniformed soldier standing under the arch with a drawn sword represents the defense of the constitution. The date 1776, the year of the Declaration of Independence, appears at the bottom. The back of the seal features an image of Georgia's coast, with two ships that represent trade, and transportation within the state.

READ ABOUT

Millions of
peaches are
harvested in
Georgia each year.

CHAPTER EIGHT

ECONOMY

★

G EORGIA EARNED ITS NICKNAME, THE PEACH STATE, BECAUSE IT PRODUCES HUGE NUMBERS OF PEACHES—33,300 TONS A YEAR. Georgia is the economic powerhouse of the Southeast. It produces a wide variety of manufactured goods, from carpets and soft drinks to airplanes. Granite and other materials are mined from its earth, and the state's coastal waters yield shrimp and other shellfish. Many large, well-known businesses have their headquarters in Georgia. Let's see what Georgians produce.

DOWN ON THE FARM

Georgia's rich, red clay soil is good for farming because it holds water and nutrients. Farmland covers nearly one-third of the state. Georgia leads the nation in the production of peanuts and pecans. Its farmers produce nearly half of the peanuts and one-third of the pecans in the United States. Georgia is also a leading fruit grower. Peaches, apples, blueberries, cantaloupes, grapes, pears, and watermelons are the state's biggest fruit crops.

Georgia ranks third in the United States in the amount of land devoted to growing vegetables. It's a major producer of collard and turnip greens, cucumbers, and lima beans. Other major vegetable crops grown by Georgia farmers are bell peppers, cabbage, corn, snap beans, sweet potatoes, and tomatoes.

Georgia's farmers grow a lot of soybeans, wheat, and tobacco. Although cotton is no longer king in Georgia, the state ranks third in the country in cotton production. Its farmers produce about 25 million bushels each year.

LIVESTOCK AND SEAFOOD

James Oglethorpe brought the first beef and dairy cows to Georgia in the 1730s. By the 1930s, the dairy industry was an important part of the state's economy. About 10 percent of the state's farmland is devoted to pastures for livestock.

SWEET AS AN . . . ONION?

In 1931, Georgia farmer Mose Coleman discovered that his onions tasted sweet rather than strong like other onions. At first, he had trouble selling his sweet onions—who had ever heard of a sweet onion? But people liked them, and Coleman's onions soon began selling at a higher price than regular onions. Other farmers in the area started growing onions, too, and they all tasted sweet. They sold their onions at a farmers' market in the nearby town of Vidalia, and the sweet onions became known as Vidalia onions.

Today, Vidalia onions are Georgia's official state vegetable. Under state law, these onions can only be grown in 20 Georgia counties, which have the right type of soil. About $90 million worth of Vidalia onions are sold each year.

Vidalia onion

Major Agricultural and Mining Products

This map shows where Georgia's major agricultural and mining products come from. See a tree? That means forest products are grown there.

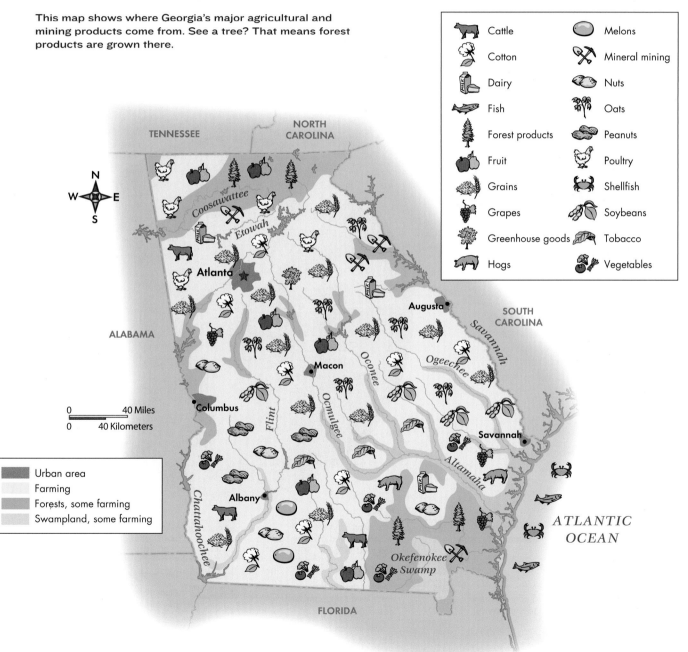

Cattle		Melons	
Cotton		Mineral mining	
Dairy		Nuts	
Fish		Oats	
Forest products		Peanuts	
Fruit		Poultry	
Grains		Shellfish	
Grapes		Soybeans	
Greenhouse goods		Tobacco	
Hogs		Vegetables	

Urban area
Farming
Forests, some farming
Swampland, some farming

0   40 Miles
0   40 Kilometers

TENNESSEE

NORTH CAROLINA

Coosawattee

Etowah

Atlanta

ALABAMA

Augusta

SOUTH CAROLINA

Savannah

Macon

Oconee

Ogeechee

Ocmulgee

Columbus

Flint

Savannah

Albany

Altamaha

Chattahoochee

Okefenokee Swamp

ATLANTIC OCEAN

FLORIDA

Top Products

Agriculture Chickens, cotton, eggs, peanuts

Manufacturing Food and beverages, transportation equipment, chemicals

Mining Kaolin, granite

Fishing Shrimp, crabs, clams

The Spanish brought hogs to Florida in 1539. Some of the animals escaped and found their way to Georgia. They soon became a popular source of food. Today, there are about 155,000 hogs statewide. Wild hogs are often seen in Georgia's coastal areas. They are considered a nuisance because they eat crops, carry diseases harmful to other livestock, and damage natural habitats.

What Do Georgians Do?

This color-coded chart shows what industries Georgians work in.

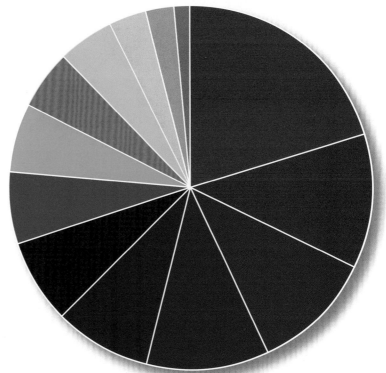

20.4% Educational services, and health care and social assistance, 873,918

11.8% Retail trade, 507,318

11.0% Professional, scientific, and management, and administrative and waste management services, 470,531

10.9% Manufacturing, 466,714

8.6% Arts, entertainment, and recreation, and accommodation and food services, 369,726

7.4% Construction, 318,753

6.4% Finance and insurance, and real estate and rental and leasing, 276,239

6.0% Transportation and warehousing, and utilities, 257,832

5.3% Public administration, 229,440

5.0% Other services, except public administration, 215,345

3.3% Wholesale trade, 140,068

2.6% Information, 113,553

1.2% Agriculture, forestry, fishing and hunting, and mining, 49,487

Source: U.S. Census Bureau, 2010 census

Georgia produces more chickens and eggs than any other state. Poultry products, which also include turkeys, make up about half of all the money earned from the state's farm products each year. Gainesville proudly calls itself the poultry capital of the world.

Shrimp is the state's most valuable seafood catch. Shrimp boats based in Brunswick, Darien, and other port cities bring in more than 4 million pounds (1.8 million kg) of shrimp each year. Oysters and crabs are also caught.

MANUFACTURING INDUSTRIES

What do Georgians make? They produce everything from the carpet in your living room to the paper in your books and the soft drinks in your refrigerator.

Carpet, textile, and cloth manufacturing have a long history in Georgia. Dalton is the "carpet capital of the world." The world's four largest carpet companies are located in Georgia. They produce more than 80 percent of the carpets made in the United States. Georgia's carpet industry employs more than 30,000 workers.

Georgia has many companies that make products from trees. Lumber mills produce wood products, and pulp mills make paper and cardboard. Georgia-Pacific, which started in Augusta in 1927, is the second-largest maker of paper products in the United States. It also makes building supplies, such as lumber, plywood, and paneling.

Georgia produces an average of nearly 18 million pounds (8 million kg) of chicken each day.

NAVAL STORES

Nope, naval stores aren't shops where you can buy anchors and life jackets. Not even close. Naval stores are products made from pine trees, such as turpentine, rosin, wood tar, and pitch. They are called naval stores because many of them were originally used to make and repair wooden ships. Turpentine is an oily substance used as a cleaner or paint thinner. Rosin is a substance used in glue, soap, and chewing gum. Violinists use rosin on bows to help the bows grip the strings of the instruments. Baseball pitchers use rosin on their fingers so they can grip the ball better. Wood tar and pitch are used to prevent water leaks in boats and on house roofs.

Because of its many pine forests, Georgia became the nation's leading naval stores producer in the 1890s. Two types of Georgia pines—longleaf and slash—produce the sticky substance called gum, which is used to make naval stores. To harvest the valuable gum, workers would cut a hole in the bark of trees and collect the gum that flowed out. As a result, however, many of Georgia's pine forests were destroyed. By 1960, Georgia's naval store industry had declined, because the pine forests were disappearing and because competing products were invented.

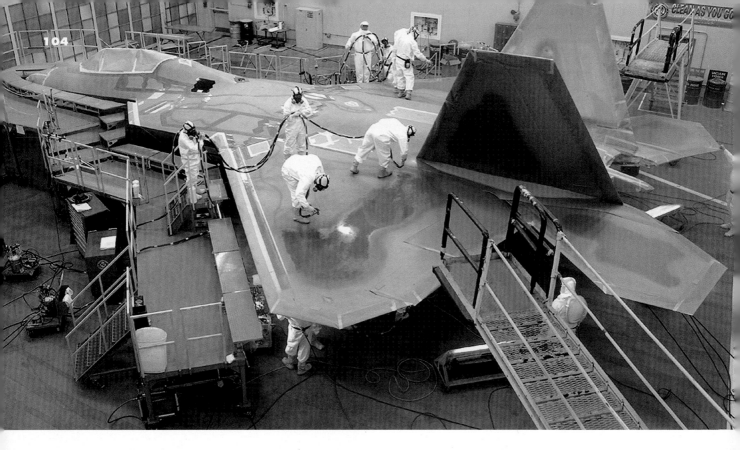

Workers at a Lockheed Martin plant in Marietta, Georgia, build a jet.

Since World War II, Georgia has been a leading aircraft manufacturing state. Beginning in 1942, Bell Aircraft built bombers at its Marietta plants. Lockheed Corporation took over the plant in the 1950s and became a major employer in the area. In 1995, Lockheed merged with nearby Martin Marietta, a company that made missiles and other weapons. Today, Lockheed Martin makes military aircraft such as the F-22 fighter and the C-130 Hercules, a large military transport plane.

Savannah's Gulfstream produces small jets often used by corporations and governments. Maule Air, based in Moultrie, makes a special type of airplane. Their small, single-engine planes need little space to take off or land. They're very popular for landing on lakes or on small airstrips in jungles or other heavily wooded areas.

MINING

Businesses that take materials out of Georgia's earth also contribute to its economy. Most of the country's kaolin (pronounced KAY-uh-lun) comes from Georgia. Kaolin is a white, chalky clay used to make paper, china, and paints. Mines in southwestern Georgia produce bauxite, which is used to make aluminum. Granite and marble are found in northern Georgia. Granite from Georgia was used to build the U.S. Capitol. Other minerals mined in Georgia include barite, feldspar, limestone, and mica.

Workers mine limestone in rural Georgia.

The CNN newsroom in Atlanta

BIG BUSINESS

About 400 of the 500 largest U.S. corporations have offices or factories in Georgia. Georgia is also the headquarters of many well-known companies. UPS has been based in Atlanta since 1991. The company delivers more than 13 million packages a day.

Home Depot was founded in Atlanta in 1978. With stores in all 50 states, it's the world's largest home-improvement business and the second-largest retailer in the United States. Delta Airlines is headquartered at Atlanta's Hartsfield-Jackson International Airport. It's the nation's third-largest airline. Turner Broadcasting is based in Atlanta. Its cable channels include Cable News Network (CNN), Cartoon Network, Turner

Network Television (TNT), and Turner Classic Movies (TCM). The Weather Channel's studios and offices are also located in Atlanta.

The best-known Georgia business of all is the Coca-Cola Company. A Georgian **pharmacist** named John Stith Pemberton invented the soft drink in 1886 and started selling it at an Atlanta drugstore. It quickly became one of the most popular products in the world. The Coca-Cola Company has had a great impact on Georgia. The company and its leaders have contributed millions of dollars to Emory University and other organizations. The Woodruff Art Center in Atlanta was built with money donated by Robert Woodruff, the head of Coca-Cola from 1926 to 1985.

A sculpture in front of the Woodruff Arts Center theater

WORD TO KNOW

pharmacist *a person who prepares and dispenses drugs and medicines*

MINI-BIO

JOHN STITH PEMBERTON: MR. COCA-COLA

John Stith Pemberton (1831–1888) was a highly respected pharmacist who invented Coca-Cola in 1886. Born in Knoxville, Georgia, he studied medicine and pharmacy in Macon. He became interested in herbal remedies (medicines made from plants) and set up a laboratory in Atlanta. He was an expert chemist, and he refined the formula for Coca-Cola in his lab. Pemberton claimed that the beverage aided digestion, gave energy to the lungs, and strengthened the muscular and nervous systems. He died two years after inventing the soft drink. The Coca-Cola formula was sold to an Atlanta businessman, and Pemberton's soft drink soon became known around the world.

? **Want to know more?** Visit www.factsfornow.scholastic.com and enter the keyword **Georgia**.

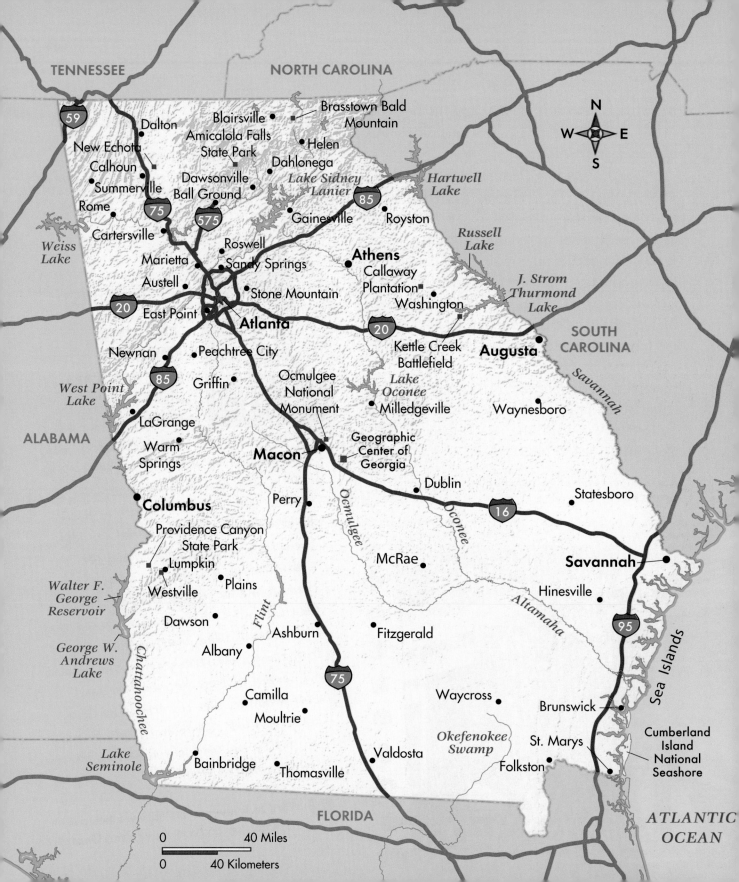

TENNESSEE

NORTH CAROLINA

59

Dalton

Blairsville

Brasstown Bald
Mountain

New Echota

Amicalola Falls
State Park

Helen

Calhoun

Dahlonega

Summerville

Dawsonville

*Lake Sidney
Lanier*

*Hartwell
Lake*

Rome

Ball Ground

75

575

Gainesville

Royston

85

Cartersville

*Weiss
Lake*

Roswell

*Russell
Lake*

Marietta

Sandy Springs

Athens

Austell

Callaway
Plantation

*J. Strom
Thurmond
Lake*

20

Stone Mountain

East Point

Washington

Atlanta

20

Newnan

Peachtree City

Kettle Creek
Battlefield

Augusta

**SOUTH
CAROLINA**

ALABAMA

85

Griffin

Ocmulgee
National
Monument

*Lake
Oconee*

Milledgeville

Savannah

LaGrange

Waynesboro

*West Point
Lake*

Warm
Springs

Geographic
Center of
Georgia

Ocmulgee

Macon

Columbus

Perry

Dublin

Statesboro

16

Oconee

Providence Canyon
State Park

McRae

Savannah

*Walter F.
George
Reservoir*

Lumpkin

Plains

Hinesville

Westville

Altamaha

*George W.
Andrews
Lake*

Dawson

Flint

Chattahoochee

Ashburn

Fitzgerald

95

Albany

Sea Islands

Camilla

75

Waycross

Brunswick

Moultrie

Valdosta

*Okefenokee
Swamp*

St. Marys

Cumberland
Island
National
Seashore

*Lake
Seminole*

Bainbridge

Thomasville

Folkston

FLORIDA

**ATLANTIC
OCEAN**

N
W E
S

0   40 Miles

0   40 Kilometers

CHAPTER NINE

TRAVEL GUIDE

TRAVEL GUIDE

★

WITH THE APPALACHIAN MOUNTAINS IN THE NORTH, A FERTILE PLAIN ACROSS ITS CENTER, AND LUSH SEA ISLANDS HUGGING THE COAST, GEORGIA IS FULL OF DIVERSE LANDSCAPES TO EXPLORE. Atlanta is a modern, bustling city, while Savannah has a slow, relaxed pace. Georgia has meandering back roads, the mysterious Okefenokee Swamp, and so much more.

← Follow along with this travel map. We'll begin in Atlanta and travel all the way down to Savannah!

THE ATLANTA AREA

THINGS TO DO: Watch the pandas at Zoo Atlanta, catch a race at Atlanta Motor Speedway, and visit the church where Martin Luther King Jr. preached.

Atlanta

★ **Georgia Aquarium:** Atlanta is home to the largest aquarium in the world, which holds more than 100,000 fish.

★ **Martin Luther King Jr. sites:** Take a tour of the Martin Luther King Jr. National Historic Site, the house where the civil rights leader was born. One block away is Ebenezer Baptist Church, where King delivered sermons as the church's pastor. Next door, you can visit King's grave at the Martin Luther King Jr. Center for Nonviolent Social Change. The inscription on his tomb comes from his "I Have a Dream" speech: "Free at last, free at last, thank God Almighty, I'm free at last."

★ **Zoo Atlanta:** This is considered one of the country's best zoos. It features pandas, gorillas, and much more.

A panda at Zoo Atlanta

★ **Georgia State Capitol:** The capitol is home to the Georgia Capitol Museum and the Georgia Hall of Fame. And don't forget to look for the gold dome on top of the capitol.

★ **Margaret Mitchell House and Museum:** Visitors can tour the apartment where Mitchell wrote *Gone with the Wind* and the movie museum with artifacts connected to the blockbuster movie of the same name.

★ **Grant Park:** The city's oldest park offers 131 acres (53 ha) of green, open space to relax. The Cyclorama, a large circular painting depicting the Battle of Atlanta, is located in Grant Park.

★ **High Museum of Art:** The Southeast's leading art museum hosts major traveling art exhibitions and has an impressive permanent collection. The building itself is a work of art, praised for its design.

★ **Atlanta Motor Speedway:** Hear the roar of race cars as they zoom around the track.

★ **World of Coca-Cola:** Sip samples of Coca-Cola products from countries around the world and see more than 100 years of Coke artifacts and memorabilia.

★ **Underground Atlanta:** Shop, eat, and enjoy entertainment at this historic underground complex.

Stone Mountain

★ **Stone Mountain State Park:** One side of Stone Mountain features the carved figures of three Confederate leaders: President Jefferson Davis, General Robert E. Lee, and General Thomas "Stonewall" Jackson. It is the world's largest **bas-relief sculpture**.

WORD TO KNOW

bas-relief sculpture *a type of sculpture in which the image is carved and projects slightly from a flat plane*

Stone Mountain

★ **Stone Mountain Park:** This popular theme park located right beside Stone Mountain features rides and shows.

THE MOUNTAINS

THINGS TO DO: Pan for gold, enjoy some German food, or climb an American Indian mound.

Blairsville

★ **Brasstown Bald Mountain:** You can see three states—Georgia, Tennessee, and North Carolina— from atop Georgia's highest point.

TEN MUST-SEE ATTRACTIONS IN GEORGIA

USA Today suggests the following popular attractions if you're planning a visit to the Peach State: Stone Mountain Park, Pebble Hill Plantation, Amicalola Falls, Jekyll Island, Chattahoochee-Oconee National Forest, the Georgia Aquarium, Sea Island Golf Club, Monterey Square, the Fox Theatre, and the Martin Luther King Jr. National Historic Site.

Dahlonega

★ **Consolidated Gold Mine:** Pan for gold at the site of America's first gold rush.

Helen

★ **Alpine Helen:** Visit a town that looks like a village from the mountainous Bavaria region of Germany. In the spring, you can cheer on your favorite balloon at Helen's hot-air balloon race. In the fall, pig out at the town's traditional German Oktoberfest.

Dawsonville

★ **Amicalola Falls State Park:** Georgia's highest waterfall plunges 729 feet (222 m) in this park.

Amicalola Falls State Park

Calhoun

★ **New Echota Historic Site:** The former capital (1825–1838) of the Cherokee Nation features original and restored buildings including the council house, the courthouse, and a store, as well as smoke-houses and corncribs.

Cartersville

★ **Etowah Indian Mounds Historic Site:** When you climb the thousand-year-old Etowah Indian Mounds, think about what it was like to live there before the arrival of Europeans.

SEE IT HERE!

TY COBB MUSEUM

Royston is home to the Ty Cobb Museum, which features exhibits celebrating the career of the Hall of Fame baseball player. Ty Cobb was born in Banks County and played for the semi-pro Royston Reds. He went on to play for the major league Detroit Tigers and Philadelphia Athletics, winning a record 12 batting titles. Cobb later donated money to build a hospital in Royston and to fund scholarships for northern Georgia students. His nickname was the Georgia Peach.

THE PIEDMONT PLATEAU

THINGS TO DO: Visit historic sites, watch some great golfers, and admire beautiful cherry blossoms.

Washington

★ **Kettle Creek Battlefield:** You can retrace the steps of soldiers at the site of an important Patriot victory during the American Revolution.

★ **Callaway Plantation:** The plantation features exhibits showing what life was like when King Cotton ruled Georgia and offers a glimpse into how enslaved people lived and worked.

Augusta

★ **Masters Tournament:** If you can get tickets, you can watch golf's greatest players at this tournament (held in early April).

Masters Tournament at Augusta National Golf Club

★ **Augusta Cotton Exchange Building:** This building dates to 1836. It is now a bank, though you can still visit the building to see an exhibit on Georgia's cotton culture.

Macon

★ **Ocmulgee National Monument:** Don't miss the chance to climb Native American mounds that may date back 8,000 years.

★ **Georgia Sports Hall of Fame:** Learn about Georgia's greatest athletes, including Hank Aaron, Sugar Ray Robinson, and Nancy Lopez, and take a look at the more than 3,000 artifacts.

★ **Cherry Trees:** Visit Macon at the right time in spring, and you'll see 60,000 blooming cherry trees.

Macon's Cherry Blossom Festival

The Southern Museum in Kennesaw celebrates the dramatic story of railroads during the American Civil War. The museum's number-one attraction is the *General*, the first train that was ever hijacked!

THE COASTAL PLAIN

THINGS TO DO: Gaze at gullies, learn about the civil rights movement, and take a picture of a giant peanut.

Lumpkin

★ **Providence Canyon State Outdoor Recreation Area:** Check out the "Little Grand Canyon." It's actually a series of huge gullies, some as deep as 150 feet (46 m), caused by erosion.

Providence Canyon

A basket weaver at Westville

★ **Westville:** Go back in time at this re-creation of an 1850 Georgia village. You can watch cobblers make shoes, smell food cooked on an open hearth, and listen to musicians playing traditional instruments.

Ashburn

★ **World's Largest Peanut:** You can't miss the World's Largest Peanut, a giant sculpture that sits atop a brick tower.

Albany

★ **Albany Civil Rights Institute:** This museum is located at Mount Zion Baptist Church, where civil rights groups met throughout the 1960s to plan protests against segregation.

THE COAST

THINGS TO DO: See alligators in the Okefenokee Swamp, enjoy the natural beauty of Cumberland Island, and take a walking tour through Savannah's historic district.

Folkston

★ **Okefenokee Swamp:** Explore one of the most unusual places in the United States. During a boat tour on the swamp's murky waters, you might spot alligators, snakes, and otters. And don't miss walking on a wiggly peat bog.

Okefenokee Swamp

St. Marys

★ **Cumberland Island National Seashore:** Here you can hike through undisturbed forests, collect shark teeth and empty seashells on the beach, or set up a telescope at night for some spectacular stargazing.

Savannah

★ **Andrew Low House:** In this historic home, Juliette Gordon Low founded the Girl Scouts of America in 1912. The house now serves as the headquarters of the Girl Scouts organization.

★ **Savannah Historic District:** Savannah is one of the most charming cities in the United States. Georgia's founder, James Oglethorpe, laid out its streets and squares. Savannah has the nation's largest historic district, with more than 1,100 historic houses and buildings.

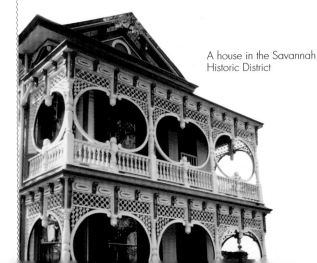

A house in the Savannah Historic District

WRITING PROJECTS

Check out these ideas for creating campaign brochures, writing you-are-there editorials, and researching explorers of the state.

ART PROJECTS

Create a great PowerPoint presentation, illustrate the state song, or learn about the state quarter and design your own.

TIMELINE

What happened when? This timeline highlights important events in the state's history—and shows what was happening throughout the United States at the same time.

FAST FACTS

Use this section to find fascinating facts about state symbols, land area and population statistics, weather, sports teams, and much more.

GLOSSARY

Remember the Words to Know from the chapters in this book? They're all collected here.

SCIENCE, TECHNOLOGY, ENGINEERING, & MATH PROJECTS

120

Make weather maps, graph population statistics, and research endangered species that live in the state.

PRIMARY VS. SECONDARY SOURCES

121

So what are primary and secondary sources? And what's the diff? This section explains all that and where you can find them.

BIOGRAPHICAL DICTIONARY

133

This at-a-glance guide highlights some of the state's most important and influential people. Visit this section and read about their contributions to the state, the country, and the world.

RESOURCES

Books and much more. Take a look at these additional sources for information about the state.

138

WRITING PROJECTS

Write a Memoir, Journal, or Editorial for Your School Newspaper!

Picture Yourself . . .

★ Building a wattle and daub house. Describe how you chose its location, then what materials you gather to make it, and finally, how you and your friends frame and complete the structure.
SEE: Chapter Two, page 26.

★ Being in Georgia during the Civil War. Imagine living in Atlanta when Union troops captured it. Describe what you see and hear.
SEE: Chapter Four, pages 49–54.

An artist's depiction of Union forces capturing Atlanta in 1864

Create an Election Brochure or Web Site!

Run for office!

Throughout this book, you've read about some of the issues that concern Georgia today. As a candidate for governor of Georgia, create a campaign brochure or Web site. Explain how you meet the qualifications to be governor of Georgia, and talk about the three or four major issues you'll focus on if you are elected. Remember, you'll be responsible for Georgia's budget. How would you spend the taxpayers' money?
SEE: Chapter Seven, pages 84–95.

Compare and Contrast —When, Why, and How Did They Come?

Compare the migration and explorations of Georgia's early Native people and its first European explorers. Tell about:

★ When their migrations began
★ How they traveled
★ Why they migrated
★ Where their journeys began and ended
★ What they found when they arrived
SEE: Chapters Two and Three, pages 22–39.

ART PROJECTS

Create a PowerPoint Presentation or Visitors' Guide

Welcome to Georgia!

Georgia's a great place to visit and to live! From its natural beauty to its bustling cities and historic sites, there's plenty to see and do. In your PowerPoint presentation or brochure, highlight 10 to 15 of Georgia's amazing landmarks. Also include:

★ a map of the state showing where these sites are located

★ photos, illustrations, Web links, natural history facts, geographic stats, climate and weather info, and descriptions of plants and wildlife.

SEE: Chapter Nine, pages 109–115.

Illustrate the Lyrics to the Georgia State Song

("Georgia on My Mind")

Use markers, paints, photos, collages, colored pencils, or computer graphics to illustrate the lyrics to "Georgia on My Mind," the state song. Turn your illustrations into a picture book, or scan them into a PowerPoint and add music.

SEE: The lyrics to "Georgia on My Mind," on page 128.

Research Georgia's State Quarter

From 1999 to 2008, the U.S. Mint introduced new quarters commemorating each of the 50 states in the order that they were admitted to the Union. Each state's quarter features a unique design on its reverse, or back.

GO TO: www.factsfornow.scholastic.com. Enter the keyword **Georgia** and look for the link to the Georgia quarter.

Research and write an essay explaining:

★ the significance of each image

★ who designed the quarter

★ who chose the final design

Design your own Georgia state quarter. What images would you choose for the reverse?

Make a poster showing the Georgia quarter and label each image.

SCIENCE, TECHNOLOGY, ENGINEERING, & MATH PROJECTS

Graph Population Statistics!

★ Compare population statistics (such as ethnic background, birth, death, and literacy rates) in Georgia counties or major cities.

★ In your graph or chart, look at population density. Write sentences describing what the population statistics show, graph one set of population statistics, and write a paragraph explaining what the graphs reveal.

SEE: Chapter Six, pages 72–75.

Create a Weather Map of Georgia!

Use your knowledge of Georgia's geography to research and identify conditions that result in specific weather events. What is it about the geography of Georgia that makes it vulnerable to things like hurricanes? Create a weather map or poster that shows the weather patterns over the state. Include a caption explaining the technology used to measure various weather phenomena, and provide data.

SEE: Chapter One, pages 16–17.

Piping plover

Track Endangered Species

★ Using your knowledge of Georgia's wildlife, research which animals and plants are endangered or threatened. Find out what the state is doing to protect these species.

★ Chart known populations of the animals and plants, and report on changes in certain geographical areas

SEE: Chapter One, page 18.

PRIMARY VS. SECONDARY SOURCES

What's the Diff?

Your teacher may require at least one or two primary sources and one or two secondary sources for your assignment. So, what's the difference between the two?

★ **Primary sources are original.** You are reading the actual words of someone's diary, journal, letter, autobiography, or interview. Primary sources can also be photographs, maps, prints, cartoons, news/film footage, posters, first-person newspaper articles, drawings, musical scores, and recordings. By the way, when you conduct a survey, interview someone, shoot a video, or take photographs to include in a project, you are creating primary sources!

★ **Secondary sources are what you find in encyclopedias, textbooks, articles, biographies, and almanacs.** These are written by a person or group of people who tell about something that happened to someone else. Secondary sources also recount what another person said or did. This book is an example of a secondary source.

Now that you know what primary sources are—where can you find them?

★ **Your school or local library:** Check the library catalog for collections of original writings, government documents, musical scores, and so on. Some of this material may be stored on microfilm.

★ **Historical societies:** These organizations keep historical documents, photographs, and other materials. Staff members can help you find what you are looking for. History museums are also great places to see primary sources firsthand.

★ **The Internet:** There are lots of sites that have primary sources you can download and use in a project or assignment.

TIMELINE

★ ★ ★

U.S. Events `1500` **Georgia Events**

1565
Spanish admiral Pedro Menéndez de Avilés founds St. Augustine, Florida, the oldest continuously occupied European settlement in the continental United States.

`1700`

1566
Spanish admiral Pedro Menéndez de Avilés explores the Georgia coast.

c. 1700
The Creek and Cherokee nations had formed.

1721
Fort King George, the first British settlement in Georgia, is built.

Fort King George

1732
King George II grants a charter for the colony of Georgia.

1733
James Oglethorpe and 120 colonists arrive in Georgia.

1750
Slavery is legalized in Georgia.

1755–63
England and France fight over North American colonial lands in the French and Indian War. By the end of the war, France has ceded all of its land west of the Mississippi to Spain and its Canadian territories to England.

Button Gwinnett, signer of the Declaration of Independence

1776
Thirteen American colonies declare their independence from Great Britain.

1776
Three Georgians sign the Declaration of Independence.

U.S. Events

Georgia Events

1782
The British leave Georgia forever.

1787
The U.S. Constitution is written.

1788
Georgia becomes the fourth state.

1793
Eli Whitney invents the cotton gin, which helps make cotton farming profitable.

1800

1803
The Louisiana Purchase almost doubles the size of the United States.

1838
The U.S. government forces the Cherokees to leave Georgia in what is known as the Trail of Tears.

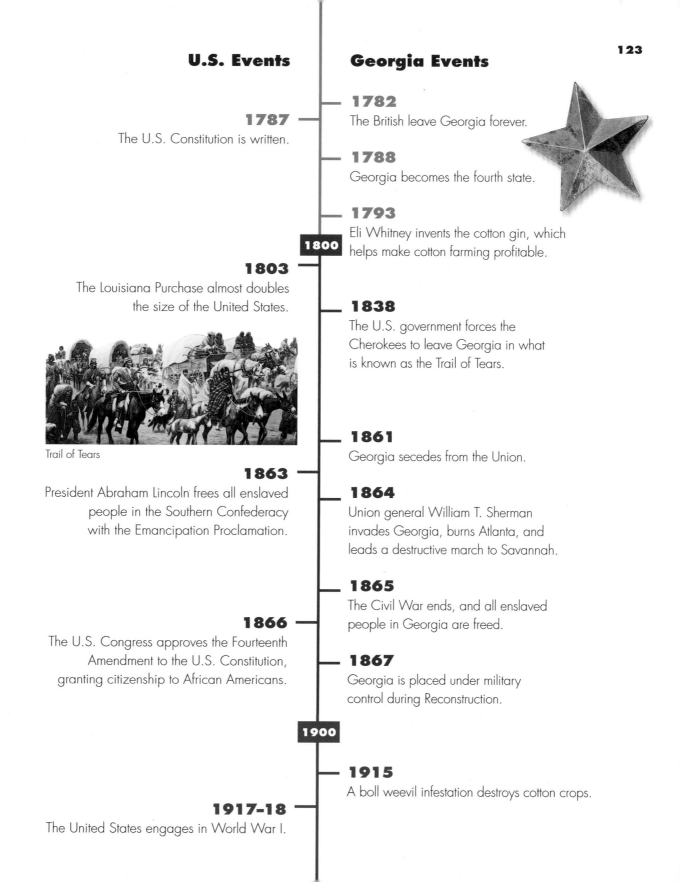

Trail of Tears

1861
Georgia secedes from the Union.

1863
President Abraham Lincoln frees all enslaved people in the Southern Confederacy with the Emancipation Proclamation.

1864
Union general William T. Sherman invades Georgia, burns Atlanta, and leads a destructive march to Savannah.

1865
The Civil War ends, and all enslaved people in Georgia are freed.

1866
The U.S. Congress approves the Fourteenth Amendment to the U.S. Constitution, granting citizenship to African Americans.

1867
Georgia is placed under military control during Reconstruction.

1900

1915
A boll weevil infestation destroys cotton crops.

1917-18
The United States engages in World War I.

U.S. Events

1929
The stock market crashes, plunging the United States more deeply into the Great Depression.

1941–45
The United States engages in World War II.

1950–53
The United States engages in the Korean War.

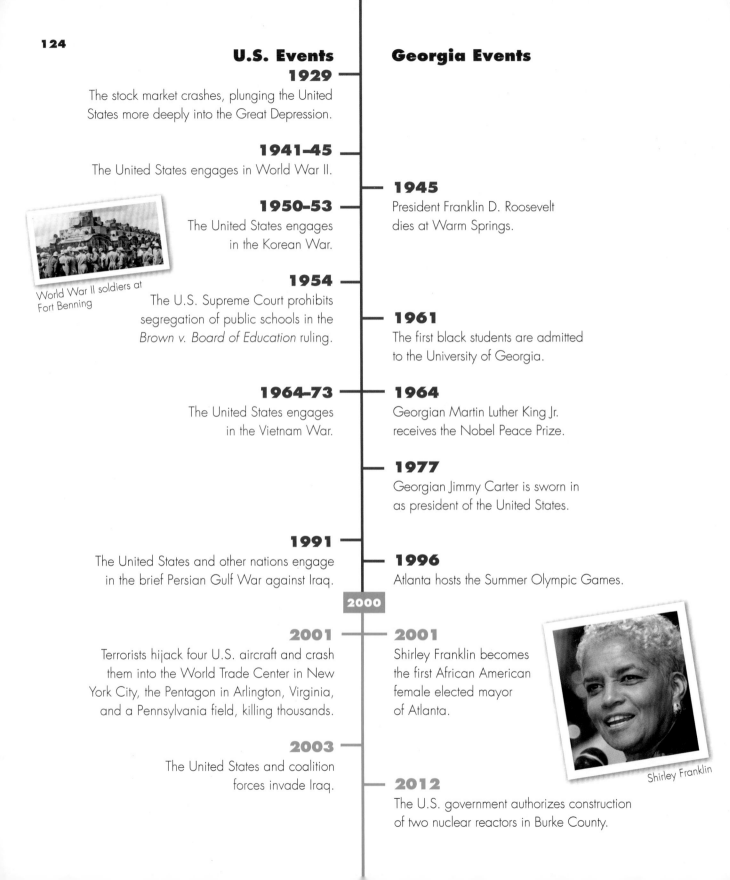

World War II soldiers at Fort Benning

1954
The U.S. Supreme Court prohibits segregation of public schools in the *Brown v. Board of Education* ruling.

1964–73
The United States engages in the Vietnam War.

1991
The United States and other nations engage in the brief Persian Gulf War against Iraq.

2000

2001
Terrorists hijack four U.S. aircraft and crash them into the World Trade Center in New York City, the Pentagon in Arlington, Virginia, and a Pennsylvania field, killing thousands.

2003
The United States and coalition forces invade Iraq.

Georgia Events

1945
President Franklin D. Roosevelt dies at Warm Springs.

1961
The first black students are admitted to the University of Georgia.

1964
Georgian Martin Luther King Jr. receives the Nobel Peace Prize.

1977
Georgian Jimmy Carter is sworn in as president of the United States.

1996
Atlanta hosts the Summer Olympic Games.

2001
Shirley Franklin becomes the first African American female elected mayor of Atlanta.

Shirley Franklin

2012
The U.S. government authorizes construction of two nuclear reactors in Burke County.

GLOSSARY

★ ★ ★

abolitionists people who work to end slavery

appeals legal proceedings in which a court is asked to change the decision of a lower court

archaeologists people who study the remains of past human societies

artifacts objects remaining from a particular period of time

bales large bundles tied together tightly for shipping or storage

barrier islands islands that are created by the gradual buildup of sand and stones from the ocean floor

bas-relief sculpture a type of sculpture in which the image is carved and projects slightly from a flat plane

bog an area of wet, marshy ground where the soil consists mostly of decomposing plant material

boycott the organized refusal to use a service or buy a product, as a form of protest

civil rights basic human rights that all citizens in a society are entitled to, such as the right to vote

colony a community settled in a new land but with ties to another government

constitution a written document that contains all the governing principles of a state or country

erosion the gradual wearing away of rock or soil by physical breakdown, chemical solution, or water

folktales traditional stories handed down for generations

geologists scientists who study rocks to find out what the earth is made of and how it has changed over time

habitats places where animals or plants naturally live

immunity natural protection against disease

lynched killed by a mob without a lawful trial

pharmacist a person who prepares and dispenses drugs and medicines

secede to withdraw from a group or an organization

segregation separation from others, according to race, class, ethnic group, religion, or other factors

sit-ins acts of protest that involve sitting in racially segregated places and refusing to leave

stocks monetary investments in a company

veto to reject a proposed piece of legislation

FAST FACTS

★   ★   ★

State Symbols

Statehood date	January 2, 1788, the 4th state
Origin of state name	Named for King George II of England
State capital	Atlanta
State nicknames	Peach State, Empire State of the South
State motto	"Wisdom, justice, and moderation"
State bird	Brown thrasher
State flower	Cherokee rose
State insect	Honeybee
State butterfly	Tiger swallowtail
State marine mammal	Right whale
State crop	Peanut
State reptile	Gopher tortoise
State fish	Largemouth bass
State seashell	Knobbed whelk
State fossil	Shark tooth
State fruit	Peach
State game bird	Bobwhite quail
State wildflower	Azalea
State gem	Quartz
State mineral	Staurolite
State song	"Georgia on My Mind" (See page 128)
State tree	Live oak
State fair	Macon (September)

State seal

Geography

Total area; rank	59,425 square miles (153,909 sq km); 24th
Land; rank	57,906 square miles (149,976 sq km); 21st
Water; rank	1,519 square miles (3,933 sq km); 25th
Inland water; rank	1,016 square miles (2,631 sq km); 20th
Coastal water; rank	48 square miles (124 sq km); 19th
Territorial water; rank	455 square miles (1,178 km); 15th
Geographic center	Twiggs County, 18 miles (29 km) southeast of Macon
Latitude	30° N to 35° N
Longitude	81° W to 85° W

Highest point Brasstown Bald mountain, 4,784 feet (1,458 m)

Lowest point Sea level at the Atlantic Ocean

Largest city Atlanta

Number of counties 159

Longest river Savannah River, 350 miles (563 km)

Population

Population; rank (2010 census): 9,687,653; 9th

Density (2010 census): 167 persons per square mile (65 per sq km)

Population distribution (2010 census): 75% urban, 25% rural

Race (2010 census): White persons: 55.9%

Black persons: 30.0%

Asian persons: 3.2%

American Indian and Alaska Native persons: 0.2%

Native Hawaiian and Other
    Pacific Islander persons: 0.1%

Persons of two or more races: 1.6%

Hispanic or Latino persons: 8.8%

Persons of some other race: 0.2%

Weather

Record high temperature 112°F (45°C) at Louisville on July 24, 1953, and at Greenville on August 20, 1983

Record low temperature −17°F (−27°C) at CCC Camp F-16 on January 27, 1940

Average July temperature, Atlanta 80°F (26°C)

Average January temperature, Atlanta 43°F (6°C)

Average annual precipitation, Atlanta 50 inches (127 cm)

State flag

STATE SONG

★ ★ ★

"Georgia on My Mind"

In 1930, Stuart Gorrell penned the words and Hoagy Carmichael composed the music to
"Georgia on My Mind." In 1960, Albany-born jazz and blues singer Ray Charles made the
song his first number-one hit. It also earned him a Grammy Award. It was the first Grammy ever
awarded to a Georgian by the National Academy of Recording Arts and Sciences. In 1979,
"Georgia on My Mind" was adopted as the state song.

Melodies bring memories
That linger in my heart,
Make me think of Georgia
Why did we ever part?

Some sweet day, when blossoms fall
And all the world's a song,
I'll go back to Georgia
'Cause that's where I belong.

Georgia, Georgia, the whole day through,
Just an old sweet song keeps Georgia on my mind.
Georgia, Georgia, a song of you
Comes as sweet and clear as moonlight through the pines.

Other arms reach out to me,
Other eyes smile tenderly,
Still in peaceful dream I see
The road leads back to you.

Georgia, Georgia, no peace I find,
Just an old sweet song keeps Georgia on my mind.

NATURAL AREAS AND HISTORIC SITES

★ ★ ★

National Recreation Area
Chattahoochee River National Recreation Area is Georgia's sole national recreation area.

National Seashore
Cumberland Island National Seashore, Georgia's only national seashore, is the largest of Georgia's Golden Isles seashores.

National Scenic Trail
Appalachian National Scenic Trail extends from Maine to Georgia.

National Monuments
Georgia has three national monuments: *Fort Frederica National Monument, Fort Pulaski National Monument,* and *Ocmulgee National Monument.*

National Military Park
Georgia's *Chickamauga and Chattanooga National Military Park* memorializes the Civil War battle sites of Chickamauga and Chattanooga.

National Battlefield Park
Kennesaw Mountain National Battlefield Park is Georgia's only national battlefield park.

National Historic Sites
Georgia hosts three national historic sites: *Martin Luther King Jr. National Historic Site, Jimmy Carter National Historic Site,* and *Andersonville National Historic Site.*

National Historic Trail
Trail of Tears National Historic Trail journeys through nine states in commemoration of the survival of the Cherokee people, despite their forced removal from their homelands.

National Forests
The *Chattahoochee -Oconee National Forest* is Georgia's only national forest.

State Parks and Forests
Georgia has nearly 50 state park areas, including *Vogel State Park* and *Indian Springs State Park,* which has been operated by the state since 1825, making it perhaps the oldest state park in the nation.

SPORTS TEAMS

★ ★ ★

NCAA Teams (Division I)

Georgia Southern University *Eagles*
Georgia State University *Panthers*
Georgia Tech *Yellow Jackets*
Mercer University *Bears*
University of Georgia *Bulldogs*
Savannah State University *Tigers*

PROFESSIONAL SPORTS TEAMS

★ ★ ★

Major League Baseball
Atlanta *Braves*

National Football League
Atlanta *Falcons*

National Basketball Association
Atlanta *Hawks*

CULTURAL INSTITUTIONS

Libraries

The *University of Georgia* (Athens) houses more than 4 million volumes and an outstanding collection of historical documents.

The Georgia Historical Society Library (Savannah) preserves books, documents, photos, maps, and any other material related to Georgia's history.

Museums

Atlanta History Center is one of the nation's largest urban museums and has exhibits on the Civil War and Atlanta history.

Columbus Museum (Columbus) covers American art and the history of the region.

The *Dahlonega Gold Museum* is on the site of the first major American gold rush, which was in 1829. It contains maps, pictures, and relics from the gold rush days.

The *Georgia Capitol Museum* (Atlanta) seeks to preserve and interpret the history of the Georgia state capitol building itself.

The *Georgia Museum of Art* at the University of Georgia (Athens) has a fine collection of American art.

The *High Museum of Art* (Atlanta) has an important collection of European masters as well as early and contemporary American art.

Louvre Atlanta (Atlanta) is a partnership between the High Museum of Art and the Musée du Louvre in Paris, which brings hundreds of works of art from the Louvre's collections to Atlanta.

Tubman African American Museum (Macon) focuses on subjects such as contemporary African American art, black films, and local history.

Performing Arts

Atlanta Opera (Atlanta) puts on major opera productions and arts education programs year-round.

The *Georgia Symphony Orchestra* (Kennesaw) performs classical, jazz, and pop music.

Universities and Colleges

In 2012, Georgia had 27 public and 51 private institutions of higher learning.

ANNUAL EVENTS

January–March

Georgia Day in Savannah (February 12)

Rattlesnake & Wildlife Festival in Claxton (early March)

Cherry Blossom Festival in Macon (mid-March)

April–June

Masters Golf Tournament in Augusta (April)

Dogwood Festival in Atlanta (early April)

Thomasville Rose Show & Festival (late April)

Vidalia Onion Festival in Vidalia (April)

Blessing of the Shrimp Fleet in Brunswick (May)

July–September

Georgia Shakespeare in Atlanta (early July)

Homespun Festival in Polk County (July)

Georgia Mountain Fair in Hiawassee (August)

Arts Festival of Atlanta (mid-September)

Barnesville Buggy Days (September)

October–December

Andersonville Historic Fair in Andersonville (October)

Georgia National Fair in Perry (October)

Gold Rush Days in Dahlonega (October)

Oktoberfest Celebration in Helen (October)

Marietta Pilgrimage in Marietta (December)

The Masters Golf Tournament at Augusta National Golf Club

BIOGRAPHICAL DICTIONARY

Conrad Aiken (1889–1973) received the Pulitzer Prize for Poetry in 1930. He was born in Savannah.

Abraham Baldwin (1754–1807) signed the U.S. Constitution on behalf of Georgia. He helped establish the University of Georgia and represented Georgia in the U.S. House of Representatives (1790–1799) and the U.S. Senate (1799–1807).

Julian Bond See page 88.

Jim Brown (1936–) is a National Football League (NFL) Hall of Famer and Hollywood actor. He played his entire nine-year career for the Cleveland Browns and won the NFL Championship in 1964. In 2002, *Sporting News* magazine named him the greatest professional football player of all time.

Erskine Caldwell (1903–1987) wrote the best-selling novels *Tobacco Road* and *God's Little Acre*. His works focused on rural life in the South. He was born in White Oak.

James Earl "Jimmy" Carter See page 89.

Ray Charles (1930–2004) was born in Albany and became an internationally acclaimed recording star. Charles began losing his sight at age five, but learned to play the piano and became a professional musician at age 15.

Ty Cobb

Ty Cobb (1886–1961), born in Narrows, was one of the greatest baseball players of all time. During his more than 23 years in the major leagues, he set records for the highest career batting average, most career hits, and most career runs, among others. He was inducted into the Baseball Hall of Fame in 1936.

William and Ellen Craft See page 49.

Ray Charles

Laurence Fishburne

Jermaine Dupri (1972–) is a Grammy Award–winning music producer. He owns his own record label, So So Def Records, and has worked with hip-hop artists such as Jay-Z, Ludacris, and Bow Wow and pop singers Mariah Carey, Usher, and others. Dupri is the youngest person to be inducted into the Georgia Music Hall of Fame. He lives in Atlanta.

Laurence Fishburne (1961–) is a movie and TV actor and director best known for his roles in the Matrix films and the cult classics *Boyz n the Hood* and *Deep Cover*. Born in Augusta, he has also appeared in Broadway stage shows, winning a Tony Award for his performance in *Two Trains Running*.

Shirley Franklin See page 95.

John C. Frémont (1813–1890) was an explorer and politician best known for his exploration of the Rocky Mountains and Pacific Coast. He served in the U.S. Army during the Mexican–American War (1846–1848) and as military governor of and U.S. senator from California. In 1856, he ran unsuccessfully for president as an antislavery candidate. He was born in Savannah.

Faye Gibbons (1939–) is the author of many children's books set in Georgia, including *Hook Moon Night*. Born in the mountains of Georgia, she lived in several towns in Georgia when she was growing up.

Grace Towns Hamilton (1907–1992) was born in Atlanta and was the first African American woman elected to the Georgia General Assembly in 1965. She served for 18 years.

Joel Chandler Harris (1848–1908) was a writer best known for his stories based on the folktales of Georgia's African Americans. His Uncle Remus stories featured characters such as Uncle Remus and Brer Rabbit. He was born in Eatonton and worked as a journalist in Atlanta.

John Henry "Doc" Holliday (1851–1887) was a gambler and gunfighter of the American Old West known for his friendship with lawman Wyatt Earp and for his role in the Gunfight at the O.K. Corral. He was born in Griffin, Georgia.

Charlayne Hunter-Gault See page 67.

Joel Chandler Harris

Maynard Jackson

Maynard Jackson (1938–2003) served as mayor of Atlanta (1974–1981, 1990–1994). He moved to Atlanta at age seven and graduated from Atlanta's Morehouse College. He was the city's first black mayor.

Bobby Jones (1902–1971) was born in Atlanta and is considered to be one of the greatest golfers ever to compete in the game. Not only a skilled golfer, he exemplified the principles of sportsmanship. The U.S. Golf Association named its sportsmanship award the Bob Jones Award.

Martin Luther King Jr. (1929–1968) was the nation's foremost civil rights leader. The Atlanta-born minister championed nonviolent demonstrations. He led a series of marches to end racial segregation in Georgia and around the country. He is remembered for his impassioned speeches. In 1964, he became the youngest person ever to win the Nobel Peace Prize.

Juliette Gordon Low (1860–1927) was born in Savannah. While living in England, she became friends with Sir Robert Baden-Powell, the founder of the Boy Scouts. She founded the Girl Scouts in 1912 and built the organization into the largest volunteer group for young women.

Ludacris (1977–) is a Grammy Award–winning hip-hop performer and actor. He moved to Atlanta in his teens and later worked as a disc jockey at an Atlanta radio station. He released his first CD in 2000. He lives in Atlanta.

Carson McCullers (1917–1967) wrote about small-town life in the South. The Columbus-born writer is best known for *The Heart Is a Lonely Hunter* and *The Member of the Wedding*.

Margaret Mitchell (1900–1949) was a journalist and author, best known for her novel *Gone with the Wind*. She was born in Atlanta and grew up there.

Leon Neel See page 20.

Margaret Mitchell

Jessye Norman (1945–) was born in Augusta and is one of the great dramatic operatic sopranos. Norman earned a bachelor's degree in music from Howard University and a master's degree from the University of Michigan. She made her operatic debut at the Metropolitan Opera in New York City in 1983.

Flannery O'Connor (1925–1964) set her fictional works in the South. The Savannah-born writer is best known for *Wise Blood* and the short story collection *A Good Man Is Hard to Find.*

James Oglethorpe (1696–1785) founded the colony of Georgia. He led 120 colonists to Georgia in 1733 and established Savannah.

John Stith Pemberton See page 107.

Harriet Powers (1837–1910) was born an enslaved person near Athens. Although she is one of the best known African American quilters, only two examples of her work survive.

Julia Roberts (1967–) is one of the most successful actresses in the world. Her best-known films include *Pretty Woman, Eat Pray Love, Ocean's Eleven,* and *Ocean's Twelve.* Born in Atlanta, she is also involved in charity work and protecting the environment.

Jessye Norman

Jackie Robinson See page 82.

John Ross See page 48.

Dean Rusk (1909–1994) was the U.S. secretary of state from 1961 to 1969 under Presidents John F. Kennedy and Lyndon B. Johnson. Previously, he served in the U.S. Army during World War II, reaching the rank of colonel. He was born in Cherokee County.

Ryan Seacrest (1974–) is one of America's most popular and recognizable celebrities. He hosts TV's *American Idol* and numerous specials as well as *On Air with Ryan Seacrest,* a radio show that airs throughout the world. He is from Dunwoody.

Alexander H. Stephens (1812–1883) represented Georgia in the U.S. House of Representatives before becoming vice president of the Confederate States of America.

Michael Stipe (1960–), born in Decatur, was the lead singer and lyricist for the rock band R.E.M. from their formation in 1980 until their breakup in 2011. He studied photography and painting at the University of Georgia.

Jackie Robinson

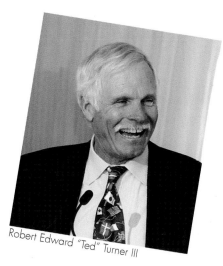

Robert Edward "Ted" Turner III

Eugene Talmadge See page 63.

Tomochichi (c. 1644–1739) was a Yamacraw chief who signed a formal treaty with James Oglethorpe that allowed the British to start a settlement at Savannah.

Robert Edward "Ted" Turner III (1939–) is a broadcasting and sports executive. He started CNN and other cable networks in Atlanta.

Alice Walker (1944–) was born in Eatonton, the child of sharecroppers. She is an acclaimed author and feminist, best known for her novel *The Color Purple*, for which she received the Pulitzer Prize for Fiction in 1983.

George Walton (1741–1804) was one of three Georgians to sign the Declaration of Independence. He later served as governor and U.S. senator.

Kanye West (1977–), gained fame as a producer for the hip-hop record company Roc-A-Fella Records. There he produced hit recordings by Jay-Z, Alicia Keyes, and Ludacris. He later became a rapper himself and recorded several top-selling albums. As a businessman, he owns a chain of restaurants and has launched fashionable lines of clothing and footwear. West was born in Atlanta.

Walter White See page 66.

Eli Whitney (1765–1825) invented the cotton gin while visiting a Savannah plantation. His invention revolutionized the cotton industry in Georgia and the South.

Joanne Woodward (1930–) was born in Thomasville. Woodward has received four Academy Award nominations for best actress and won in 1957 for *The Three Faces of Eve*. She has also won two Emmy Awards.

Trisha Yearwood (1964–) is a popular country-and-western singer. She was born in Monticello and was inducted into the Georgia Music Hall of Fame in 2000.

Andrew Young Jr. (1932–) is a civil rights leader and politician. He served as a congressman (1972–1977), U.S. ambassador to the United Nations (1977–1979), and mayor of Atlanta (1982–1990).

Alice Walker

RESOURCES

★ ★ ★

BOOKS

Nonfiction

Doak, Robin S. *Voices from Colonial America: Georgia, 1521–1776*. Washington, D.C.: National Geographic Books, 2006.

Farris, Christine King. *My Brother Martin: A Sister Remembers Growing Up with the Rev. Dr. Martin Luther King Jr.* New York: Aladdin, 2006.

Fradin, Judith Bloom. *5,000 Miles to Freedom: Ellen and William Craft's Flight from Slavery*. Washington, D.C.: National Geographic, 2006.

Seidman, David. *Jimmy Carter: President and Peacemaker*. Danbury, Conn.: Franklin Watts, 2004.

Sonneborn, Liz. *A Primary Source History of the Colony of Georgia*. New York: Rosen, 2006.

Fiction

Brady, Laurel. *Say You Are My Sister*. New York: HarperCollins, 2000.

Gibbons, Faye. *Hook Moon Night*. New York: Morrow Junior Books, 1997.

Jaquith, Priscilla. *Bo Rabbit Smart for True: Tall Tales from the Gullah*. New York: Philomel, 1995.

Kadohata, Cynthia. *Kira-Kira*. New York: Atheneum, 2004.

Murphy, Rita. *Black Angels*. New York: Delacorte, 2001.

O'Connor, Barbara. *Moonpie and Ivy*. New York: Farrar, Straus and Giroux, 2001.

Rinaldi, Ann. *Numbering All the Bones*. New York: Hyperion, 2002.

Woods, Brenda. *My Name Is Sally Little Song*. New York: Putnam, 2006.

Young, Ronder Thomas. *Moving Mama to Town*. New York: Orchard Books, 1997.

Visit this Scholastic Web site for more information on Georgia:
www.factsfornow.scholastic.com
Enter the keyword **Georgia**

AUTHOR'S TIPS AND SOURCE NOTES

★　★　★

Researching this book gave me a chance to learn more about the state. Kenneth Coleman's *A History of Georgia* was a great resource. It provided in-depth information on Georgia's history from the colonial period until the late 1970s. To learn about Georgia's Indians, I consulted general books on Native Americans, as well as books on Creeks and Cherokees. These books included Carl Waldman's *Encyclopedia of Native American Tribes* and *Atlas of the North American Indian*, Theda Perdue and Michael Green's *The Columbia Guide to American Indians of the Southeast*, Theda Perdue's *The Cherokees*, and Michael Green's *The Creeks*.

I found much more information about Georgia and its land, people, and economy in many books from the library. These books included Charles Lowery and John Marzalek's *The Greenwood Encyclopedia of African American Civil Rights*, Burke Davis's *Sherman's March*, Richard Selcer's *Civil War America*, and John Edge's *Georgia*.